Politics and Chaplaincy
IN THE COMMONWEALTH OF THE BAHAMAS

Jonathan C. Carey

CAREY PRESS
EQUIPPING ENCOURAGING EMPOWERING

Politics & Chaplaincy in the Commonwealth of the Bahamas

ISBN 979-889940011-7 Paperback

Printed in the United States of America

Advance Praise for
Politics and Chaplaincy

Chaplaincy is a specialized ministry of service intended to provide spiritual support, guidance, and counseling, not in a local church but to the public at large. It is about loving people and sharing the message of Jesus Christ, and we will only be as effective as our passion for it. Politics, however, is associated with the governance of a country or area. I have discovered as a senior pastor and chaplain that to navigate both faith and nation is a gift and requires heart, faith in God, dedication, and perseverance.

I am so grateful for my dear friend and mentor, Jonathan C. Carey, who has devoted his life to Chaplaincy and Training. When I accepted the assignment of Chaplain in 2021, I did not know what chaplaincy was until I attended one of Jonathan Carey's Chaplaincy Training Certification Courses. I have been able to effectively fulfill my mandate and assignment as Chaplain of The Royal Bahamas Defence Force in The Commonwealth of The Bahamas as a result of his mentorship and training.

Jonathan Carey's passion for Chaplaincy Training and empowering others is always evident. This, coupled with his vast knowledge and expertise in the field, certainly qualifies him to author such an indispensable and timely read. ***Politics and Chaplaincy in the Commonwealth of The Bahamas*** is a testament to his dedication to Chaplaincy and commitment to keeping it relevant while recognizing the unsung heroes of the Bahamian political landscape—the dedicated chaplains who faithfully and selflessly served the great nation of The Bahamas. This book highlights their commitment to both spiritual and civic duty and the impact they would have had on humanity.

Jonathan Carey explores the distinction between a traditional pastor and a political chaplain, exploring the unique role of chaplains. Get ready to be blessed by this enlightening and insightful read!

Chief Apostle Raymond K. Wells

—Senior Pastor, Living Waters Kingdom Ministries
—Chaplain of The Royal Bahamas Defence Force
—Frontline Chaplains International Corps Commander
for The Commonwealth of The Bahamas

Advance Praise for
Politics and Chaplaincy

Politics and Chaplaincy is a strategic work that addresses an often unspoken dilemma that pastors and chaplains face in a world of political allegiances and agendas. It is interesting to note that Jesus Himself outlined the believer's role when He stated that we should be, "In the world but not of it."

In other words, we must be strategic and aware that, no matter what country we live in, our primary citizenship is the Kingdom of God and, regardless of how we feel about politics in our environment, we must understand how to live in two worlds, advancing the principles about which Jesus spoke that represent the greatest hope of a nation.

In my time of serving as parliamentary chaplain, many tried to get me to focus on one party or the other; but the astute chaplain must understand that our job is to advance Kingdom principles that apply to all, regardless of their political affiliation. To side with or become a pawn of any political party in your role is a stain on the name of the One who called you higher as His Ambassador in the earth.

This book speaks to that delicate balance of functioning in an environment but understanding that our calling is beyond politics or personality, and we are obligated to offer Godly advice and counsel and to steer the conversation back to the principles that ensure success for the nation.

Jonathan is qualified to speak, having functioned as a global Kingdom Ambassador through tragedy and turmoil, offering hope and guidance for the common man and the significant political and civic leaders for decades. Being a chaplain is not easy, but it is vital in times of need and abundance; and we need knowledge to function effectively. This book provides that knowledge, ensuring clarity of purpose and function.

Dr. Dave Burrows

—Senior Pastor & Co-founder of
*Bahamas Faith Ministries Church**
—President & Co-founder of
*Bahamas Faith Ministries International**

**Both ministries were co-founded with*
the late world-renowned visionary and leader
Dr. Myles Munroe, whom he succeeded.

TABLE OF CONTENTS

TABLE OF CONTENTS

Dedication

This book is dedicated to the unsung heroes of the Bahamian political landscape—the dedicated chaplains, who tirelessly serve their nation with unwavering faith, compassion, and resilience.

Their unwavering commitment to both spiritual and civic duty inspires us all to strive for a more just and compassionate society. It is to their selfless service, often undertaken amidst challenging circumstances, that this work is humbly offered. Their strength, dedication, and unwavering belief in the power of service in the face of adversity serve as a beacon, guiding us towards a deeper understanding of the unique intersection of faith, politics, and community in The Bahamas. May this book serve as a testament to their profound impact and inspire others to embrace the demanding but deeply rewarding vocation of political chaplaincy. Their selfless acts of service form the bedrock upon which a stronger and more compassionate Bahamas is built. This work is a small token of gratitude for their immense contribution.

Preface

The intersection of politics and chaplaincy presents a unique and often complex landscape. This book, *Politics and Chaplaincy in the Commonwealth of The Bahamas,* emerges from a deep engagement with the realities and challenges faced by those who navigate this intricate terrain. As a seasoned chaplain with extensive experience in pastoral care and community service, I have witnessed firsthand the profound impact of faith-based leadership in the political sphere. My work with first responders and in disaster relief has underscored the crucial role of spiritual support in times of crisis, particularly within the specific context of The Bahamas.

This volume aims to provide both a theoretical framework and a practical guide for understanding and effectively engaging in political chaplaincy. It explores the delicate balance between political allegiance and broader community service, examining ethical dilemmas and offering insights into effective pastoral care strategies. The Bahamian context serves as a rich case study, allowing us to examine the historical interplay of religion and politics, while simultaneously offering transferable lessons for similar contexts around the globe. Through a combination of historical analysis, practical advice, and real-world examples, this book seeks to equip current and aspiring political chaplains, pastors, and community leaders with the knowledge and tools necessary to excel in their respective roles. My hope is that this work contributes to a more nuanced understanding of the vital contribution of faith-based leadership within the political arena. The reader will find not merely a text, but a companion in navigating the complex ethics and practicalities of this field.

Introduction

The Bahamian archipelago, with its vibrant culture and history, provides a compelling context to explore the complex and often overlooked relationship between politics and chaplaincy. This book probes into this intersection, offering an examination of the unique role of chaplains within the Bahamian political system. We will explore the crucial distinctions between the roles of a traditional pastor and a political chaplain, highlighting the specific responsibilities and challenges inherent in serving both a political party and the wider community. The presentation moves beyond abstract theory to offer practical guidance for political chaplains, emphasizing the importance of self-care, effective communication strategies, and community engagement.

We will explore how chaplains can provide crucial pastoral care to politicians and staff, as well as the essential support they offer first responders navigating high-stress situations. The historical context of The Bahamas, with its intertwined religious and political heritage, forms the backdrop for understanding the present-day realities. Through an overview of historical events, we will examine the influence of religious figures on Bahamian politics and trace the evolution of chaplaincy within the political system. Ethical considerations are central to this discussion, prompting critical reflection on potential conflicts of interest and the need to maintain impartiality while remaining true to one's faith and political allegiance.

This book will also engage in an analysis of the many facets of resource management, collaboration with other agencies, and the crucial role of effective communication. By weaving together theoretical insights with real-world examples, case studies, and practical advice, this book serves as a valuable resource for political chaplains, pastors, politicians, and anyone interested in the critical intersection of faith, politics, and community service within the

unique context of The Bahamas and beyond. The book concludes with practical resources and ethical guidelines to equip readers with the tools they need to make a meaningful contribution in this vital field.

CHAPTER 1
Historical Intersection of Religion and Politics in The Bahamas

The Bahamas, a nation steeped in a rich tapestry of colonial history and vibrant cultural heritage, presents a fascinating case study of the interwoven relationship between religion and politics. Understanding this intricate dance is crucial to grasping the contemporary role of political chaplaincy within the islands' unique societal fabric. The history of The Bahamas is, in many ways, a story of the interplay between religious belief, social movements, and the evolution of its political landscape. From its early days under British colonial rule to its eventual independence, the influence of religious denominations on political discourse and social change has been profound and multifaceted.

The early settlement of The Bahamas was significantly influenced by religious factors. While the initial waves of settlement brought with them diverse religious affiliations, the Church of England, as the established church under British rule, held a dominant position for centuries. This dominance wasn't simply a matter of numbers; it was intrinsically linked to the colonial power structure. The Church of England—referred to locally as the Anglican Church— played a vital role in governance, education, and social control, often reflecting and reinforcing the existing power dynamics. Missionaries, many affiliated with the Church of England, were integral to the colonization process, contributing to both the spiritual and socio-political landscape. Their work, while often motivated by benevolent intentions, also served to solidify British influence and control over the islands. The colonial government's close association with the Anglican Church ensured its privileged position within society, impacting not only the religious but also the social and political spheres.

However, the religious landscape was never monolithic. Other denominations, including Baptist, Methodist, and Roman Catholic churches, gradually gained a foothold in The Bahamas, often challenging the established Anglican dominance. These dissenting groups frequently became focal points for social and political activism, particularly during times of social unrest or calls for greater self-governance.

The Methodist and Baptist churches, in particular, played crucial roles in supporting movements for social reform and equality, often providing a safe haven for those marginalized or oppressed within the colonial system. Their advocacy for education, improved living conditions, and greater political rights contributed significantly to shaping the course of Bahamian history. The 19th and 20th centuries witnessed a growing awareness of the disparities within Bahamian society, fueled in part by the burgeoning strength of non-conformist religious groups. These groups, often representing the voices of the marginalized and disenfranchised, played a critical role in challenging the status quo. Their involvement in political discourse, though often subtle, was significant. Church buildings served as meeting places for political discussions and organizing efforts, while religious leaders frequently acted as moral compasses and advocates for social justice. Their influence extended beyond mere political activism; religious institutions often provided essential social services, such as education and healthcare, supplementing and sometimes challenging the colonial administration's efforts.

The process for Bahamian independence in the mid-20th century saw religious leaders playing a pivotal role. Many clergy members, representing diverse denominations, actively participated in the political campaigns leading to the nation's autonomy. They provided moral and spiritual guidance, rallied support among their congregations, and served as voices of reason and moderation during times of heightened political tension. Their involvement wasn't always uniform, reflecting the diverse political perspectives within the religious community. However, their collective contribution underscores the deep-seated intertwining of religion and politics in the struggle for self-determination.

The post-independence era has witnessed a continued engagement between religion and politics in The Bahamas. Religious institutions remain significant actors within Bahamian society, contributing to political discourse, social justice initiatives, and community development programs. While the established church still retains influence, the religious landscape has become increasingly diverse, with a greater representation of Pentecostal and other evangelical churches. This religious diversity has, in turn, influenced the political spectrum, reflecting a broader array of social and political views.

The relationship hasn't been without its complexities. The role of religion in shaping moral values and influencing political debates continues to be a point of discussion. Issues such as same-sex marriage, gender equality, abortion rights, and others have highlighted the intricate and sometimes conflicting relationships between religious beliefs and political policy. These debates, often fiercely contested, reflect the dynamic and ever-evolving nature of the interplay between religion and politics in The Bahamas. Understanding these complexities is critical in navigating the ethical and practical considerations associated with political chaplaincy.

RECAP

The colonial legacy has left an indelible mark on the relationship between religious institutions and political structures in The

Bahamas. The historical dominance of the Anglican Church, its close association with colonial power, and the subsequent rise of non-conformist denominations have shaped the contemporary religious landscape. The legacy of social inequality, rooted in both colonial and post-colonial dynamics, remains a central theme impacting the engagement of religious groups in political and social issues. It highlights the delicate balance that political chaplains must navigate between their spiritual role and their involvement in the political realm.

In conclusion, understanding the historical intersection of religion and politics in The Bahamas is paramount to comprehending the contemporary role of political chaplaincy. The nation's history, marked by a complex interplay of colonial influence, religious diversity, social movements, and evolving political structures, has shaped the current socio-political landscape. Tracing this historical journey helps illuminate the challenges and opportunities faced by political chaplains today. The examples of religious leaders who successfully navigated the complex terrain of faith and politics, as well as those whose actions raised ethical questions, provide valuable lessons for those seeking to serve in this unique and challenging vocation. This historical analysis forms a vital foundation for the subsequent discussion of the distinct roles and responsibilities of a political chaplain, the ethical considerations they face, and the strategies necessary for an effective ministry within the political sphere.

REFLECTION STEP

The fruit of the future is contained in the seeds of the past. What are some ways Political Chaplaincy can sow seeds for a more productive national political future?

REFLECTION (CONTINUED)

CHAPTER 2
Defining Political Chaplaincy Roles and Responsibilities

The preceding discussion established the deeply interwoven nature of religion and politics in the Bahamian context, tracing a historical narrative from colonial times to the present. This historical understanding provides a crucial backdrop against which to define the unique role of the political chaplain. It's vital to differentiate this role from that of a traditional pastor, for while sharing some common ground in spiritual guidance and pastoral care, their functions and responsibilities diverge significantly within the political sphere.

A traditional pastor primarily focuses on the spiritual well-being of their congregation, providing pastoral care, preaching sermons, conducting religious services, and offering spiritual counsel. Their sphere of influence is largely confined to the religious community they serve. Their role, while deeply impactful within that community, does not typically extend to navigating the complex dynamics of partisan politics or engaging directly in the political process beyond advocating for broad social justice issues.

Accountability is primarily to their congregation and the governing body of their denomination or fellowship. The political chaplain, however, operates in a vastly different arena. Their role transcends the boundaries of the traditional pastoral office, requiring a unique skill set encompassing spiritual leadership, political acumen, and exceptional interpersonal skills. While maintaining their core commitment to spiritual principles, they navigate the intricacies of the political landscape, offering pastoral care and support not just to a singular congregation, but to a broader political entity—a party, or even an entire legislative body (Parliament or Senate). This

expanded scope brings with it a broader range of responsibilities and a heightened sensitivity to potential conflicts of interest.

One of the most significant distinctions lies in the nature of their relationship with the political party they serve. Unlike a traditional pastor who serves a congregation based on shared faith, the political chaplain's relationship is built on the shared goals and values of a political party. This requires careful navigation. While providing spiritual guidance and support to party members, the chaplain must uphold their ethical integrity and avoid becoming overly partisan. Their role is not to endorse specific policies or advocate for particular political outcomes, but rather to foster unity, promote ethical conduct, and provide emotional and spiritual support within the often-stressful environment of political life. This delicate balance requires exceptional discernment and a profound understanding of the ethical considerations inherent in the role.

The community engagement of a political chaplain extends beyond their specific political affiliation. While they serve the interests of their political party, their responsibilities also encompass broader community involvement. They may offer support services to first responders, emergency personnel, or victims of both natural and man made disasters, regardless of their political leanings. This demonstrates a commitment to serving the wider community's needs, transcending the confines of partisan politics.

This aspect of their work necessitates strong organizational and leadership skills, the ability to build bridges across different communities and perspectives, and a commitment to building trust and understanding.

The ethical boundaries of political chaplaincy present significant challenges. Maintaining impartiality while working within a partisan environment necessitates a strong moral compass and a resolute commitment to ethical conduct. The political chaplain must avoid actions that could be perceived as favoring one party over another, even subtly. This requires careful consideration of their public statements, their interactions with individuals from different political backgrounds, and their engagement in community activities. Transparency is paramount and establishing clear boundaries regarding their role and responsibilities is crucial to maintaining public trust and avoiding potential conflicts of interest.

Let's consider some hypothetical scenarios to illustrate these challenges. Suppose a political chaplain's party experiences a significant electoral defeat. Their role then shifts to providing emotional support and spiritual guidance during a time of discouragement and uncertainty. They must help party members process their feelings of disappointment and loss, offering a sense of hope and resilience while remaining respectful of opposing political viewpoints. Conversely, if the party achieves victory, the chaplain must counsel against hubris and remind members of the importance of humility and service to the community.

Another scenario might involve a disagreement within the party concerning a sensitive ethical issue, such as a proposed policy with significant moral implications. The chaplain's role in this situation is not to dictate the outcome, but to facilitate respectful dialogue, promote understanding, and help the members to consider the ethical dimensions of their decisions. They might convene discussions, offer moral guidance based on their religious faith, and provide a safe space for open and honest conversation. The emphasis is on fostering ethical decision-making within the party, not on dictating policy or partisan advantage.

The unique demands of political chaplaincy necessitate a strong commitment to self-care. The emotional toll of working within a high-pressure, often contentious environment can be significant. The political chaplain must actively prioritize their own well-being to prevent burnout and maintain their effectiveness. This includes seeking personal spiritual guidance, maintaining healthy boundaries, engaging in activities that promote relaxation and stress reduction, and seeking support from peers or mentors who understand the complexities of the role. Ignoring self-care is a recipe for professional failure and personal distress, which ultimately undermines the effectiveness of their ministry within the political realm.

Furthermore, the political chaplain must develop a deep understanding of the political system, including the nuances of political strategy, the power dynamics within the party, and the broader social and cultural context within which the party operates. This understanding allows them to effectively tailor their approach to pastoral care and provide relevant support to individuals within the party. It also enhances their ability to build relationships across political divides and promote positive dialogue within the community.

Finally, the role of the political chaplain in the Bahamian context is inextricably linked to the historical and cultural influences already discussed. The legacy of colonialism, the diversity of religious traditions, and the evolving social dynamics all play a role in shaping the challenges and opportunities faced by political chaplains. Navigating these complex layers of history and culture requires sensitivity, humility, and a commitment to understanding the perspectives of different communities within Bahamian society. A successful political chaplain will be one who effectively bridges these cultural and historical divides, promoting unity and reconciliation through their ministry. Their work is not merely spiritual but fundamentally social and deeply political. Their effectiveness hinges on their ability to balance these different dimensions of their role with unwavering integrity.

REFLECTION STEP

This chapter discusses the balance a Political Chaplain should maintain for effective ministry. Please share your self-care methods and any changes you plan to implement.

REFLECTION (CONTINUED)

CHAPTER 3
The Pastor's Role vs The Political Chaplain's Role

Let's take a closer look at the differences between the roles of a pastor and chaplain. The core responsibility of traditional pastors centers on the spiritual well-being of their congregations. This involves preaching, teaching biblical principles, administering sacraments, providing counseling and pastoral care, and generally fostering a sense of community and shared faith among their flock. Their accountability lies primarily with their congregation and the governing body of their denomination or fellowship. Their work focuses on the internal life of the church, addressing individual and collective spiritual needs within a framework of established religious doctrines and practices. Ethical considerations primarily involve maintaining confidentiality within pastoral counseling, adhering to the tenets of their faith, and ensuring the responsible stewardship of church resources. While a pastor may engage in social justice advocacy, their primary focus remains on the spiritual nurture and guidance of their congregation. Their actions are guided by theological principles, and their accountability is largely internal to the religious community.

In stark contrast, the political chaplain operates within a much broader and more complex environment. While sharing a common foundation of pastoral care and spiritual guidance with the traditional pastor, their role extends significantly beyond the confines of a single religious community. Their primary constituency may be a political party, a legislative body, or a specific branch of government. This difference dramatically alters the nature of their responsibilities and the ethical considerations they must navigate.

The political chaplain's responsibilities encompass providing pastoral care and spiritual guidance to political leaders, staff, and often, even their families. This requires a deep understanding of the unique pressures and stresses inherent in political life—the intense scrutiny, the constant public pressure, the long working hours, the inherent conflicts and disagreements, and the often-unpredictable nature of the political landscape. Their role is not simply to offer solace in moments of defeat but also to provide guidance and support during periods of intense pressure and decision-making. They may be called upon to counsel individuals dealing with ethical dilemmas, navigating complex interpersonal relationships within the political environment, or coping with the emotional weight of high-stakes decisions.

Moreover, the political chaplain may also play a crucial role in fostering unity and collaboration within the political body they serve. This involves facilitating dialogue between differing factions, promoting ethical conduct among political actors, and fostering a sense of shared purpose and common values. They may organize events that promote cohesion, offer mediation services in internal conflicts, and provide a space for open communication and constructive dialogue. This necessitates exceptional interpersonal skills, a high degree of emotional intelligence, and an ability to build trust across ideological and political divides.

The ethical complexities facing a political chaplain are significantly greater than those faced by a traditional pastor. Maintaining absolute confidentiality is paramount, but the line between confidential pastoral counseling and information that might impact public policy or the reputation of their political affiliation can be blurred. Political chaplains must tread this fine line with exceptional care, meticulously ensuring that they do not breach the trust placed in them while remaining mindful of the potential implications of undisclosed information. Furthermore, the potential

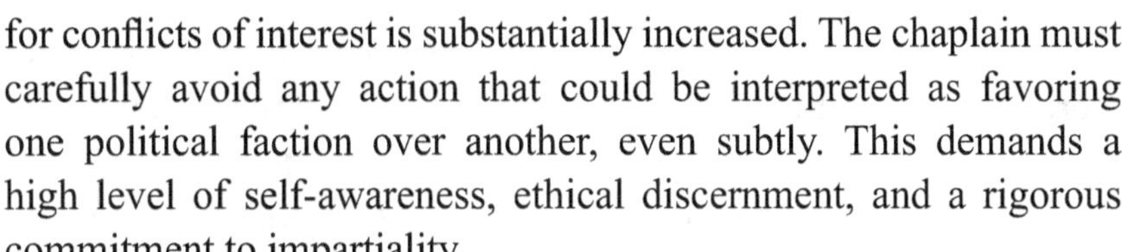

for conflicts of interest is substantially increased. The chaplain must carefully avoid any action that could be interpreted as favoring one political faction over another, even subtly. This demands a high level of self-awareness, ethical discernment, and a rigorous commitment to impartiality.

Consider the example of a political chaplain working with a legislative body facing a deeply divisive issue, such as a proposed law on a contentious social matter. The chaplain's role is not to endorse or oppose the legislation but rather to facilitate open and respectful debate, ensuring that all sides feel heard and that moral considerations are fully explored. Their influence lies in fostering constructive dialogue and promoting ethical considerations, not in dictating the outcome of the political process. This requires exceptional skill in mediation, conflict resolution, and navigating delicate interpersonal dynamics. Political chaplains must be able to listen empathetically, offer sound moral counsel based on their religious beliefs, and promote a climate of mutual respect among conflicting parties.

Another crucial aspect of a political chaplain's role involves supporting first responders and other essential personnel who may experience significant trauma and stress in the line of duty. This extends beyond the confines of their immediate political affiliation, demonstrating a commitment to serving the wider community. In the Bahamian context, following hurricanes or other natural disasters, the political chaplain might play a vital role in providing emotional and spiritual support to victims and first responders alike, often working collaboratively with other aid organizations.

This aspect of their work highlights the broader community outreach that distinguishes the political chaplain from the traditional pastor, emphasizing their role as a source of strength and resilience for the entire community.

In The Bahamas, with its unique history and complex social fabric, the role of the political chaplain is particularly nuanced. The historical influence of colonialism, the diverse religious landscape, and the ongoing socio-economic challenges all shape the context within which political chaplains operate. They must navigate these complexities with sensitivity and an understanding of the various cultural perspectives within Bahamian society. Building trust across different communities and promoting reconciliation are essential aspects of their work. Their role transcends simple spiritual guidance to encompass a broader mission of social harmony and community building.

Furthermore, successful political chaplains cultivate a deep understanding of the political system, its processes, and its dynamics. This includes familiarity with the intricacies of parliamentary procedures, the power dynamics within the political party they serve, and the broader social and political forces influencing the political landscape. This comprehensive understanding allows them to tailor their pastoral care appropriately and to engage in effective conflict resolution and mediation.

In summary, while both traditional pastors and political chaplains share a foundation in spiritual guidance and pastoral care, their roles diverge considerably in terms of context, responsibilities, and ethical considerations. The political chaplain operates within a much broader and more complex environment, demanding a unique skill set and a heightened awareness of the ethical implications of their actions. The Bahamian context adds another layer of complexity, requiring sensitivity to historical and cultural nuances. Ultimately, the effectiveness of a political chaplain rests on their ability to navigate these complexities with integrity, promoting unity, compassion, and ethical conduct within the political sphere while steadfastly attending to their own well-being. Their work is

a vital and often unseen contribution to the health and stability of the political system.

REFLECTION STEP

Give a personal example of fostering trust as a political chaplain in the community.

REFLECTION (CONTINUED)

CHAPTER 4
Ethical Considerations and Potential Conflicts of Interest

The ethical landscape for a political chaplain in The Bahamas, or indeed anywhere, is a complex and often treacherous terrain. Unlike the traditional pastor whose ethical considerations largely revolve around congregational matters and denominational or fellowship guidelines, the political chaplain operates within a dynamic sphere where personal faith, political allegiance, and community well-being constantly intersect. This intersection frequently creates potential conflicts of interest that require careful navigation and a robust ethical framework for decision-making.

One primary source of conflict stems from the inherent tension between loyalty to a political party and commitment to the broader community. Political chaplains employed by a specific party, for example, might find themselves privy to confidential information that could be used to the party's advantage, even if that advantage comes at the expense of fairness or the overall good of the community. This could manifest in various ways. Imagine a situation where a chaplain learns, during a confidential pastoral session, of a potentially damaging scandal within the opposing party. Sharing that information, even anonymously, could influence the political landscape significantly. However, maintaining confidentiality, a cornerstone of pastoral care, would demand silence. The ethical dilemma then lies in balancing loyalty to the individual, the promise of confidentiality, and the potential impact on the broader political process and the common good. There's no simple answer; the political chaplain must grapple with this conflict using sound judgment and a deeply developed moral compass, constantly reflecting on the principles of justice, fairness, and the well-being of all citizens.

Furthermore, the chaplain's role may require counseling individuals involved in deeply divisive issues, such as those related to national security, economic policy, or social justice. Maintaining neutrality and impartiality becomes paramount. The chaplain should facilitate dialogue and mediation, guiding individuals toward compromise and understanding, rather than offering partisan opinions or advocating for specific political outcomes. This impartiality must extend even to situations where the chaplain's personal beliefs strongly align with one side of the debate. Their role is not to impose their personal views but to serve as a neutral facilitator, promoting constructive dialogue and ethical decision-making across the political spectrum. Any perceived bias, regardless of the chaplain's actual intentions, can significantly erode trust and undermine effectiveness. The Bahamian context, with its own unique historical and social divisions, underscores the importance of this neutrality.

The potential for conflicts of interest extends beyond partisan politics. The political chaplain may be called upon to counsel individuals who are also significant donors to their political party or who hold considerable influence within the government. This raises concerns about the perception, and indeed the reality, of favoritism.

The chaplain must strive to maintain equitable treatment of all individuals, ensuring that their relationship with a particular individual does not influence the impartiality of their counsel or pastoral care. Transparency and established protocols for managing conflicts of interest can mitigate such concerns, but constant vigilance and self-reflection are crucial. A robust code of ethics, potentially developed in collaboration with relevant governing bodies and religious organizations, can offer guidance and framework for handling these intricate situations.

Another ethical challenge arises from the nature of political power and influence. Political chaplains, by virtue of their proximity to power, could potentially leverage their position to gain personal advantages or to advance specific agendas. This includes the subtle influence exerted through informal conversations or advice given in confidence. Maintaining ethical boundaries and resisting any temptation to exploit one's position for personal gain is paramount. Regular reflection on one's motives, alongside accountability mechanisms like mentorship or supervision, can provide crucial safeguards against abuse of power.

The use of resources also presents ethical challenges. Political chaplains might have access to resources through their political affiliation—be it funding, personnel, or logistical support—which could be used for partisan purposes. Ensuring that these resources are utilized transparently and equitably for the benefit of the whole community, not just the political party, is a crucial ethical responsibility.

The importance of transparency and accountability cannot be overstated. Developing clear and publicly accessible codes of conduct, along with mechanisms for reporting ethical breaches, is crucial for maintaining public trust and upholding the integrity of the office of political chaplain. This includes transparency in financial dealings, conflict-of-interest declarations, and the management of resources. Independent oversight bodies could also play a role in ensuring accountability and enforcing ethical standards.

Furthermore, the political chaplain must be acutely aware of the potential for burnout. The emotional demands, the constant exposure to conflict, and the pressure to maintain a delicate balance between political loyalty and community service can lead to exhaustion and disillusionment. Prioritizing self-care, including regular time

for prayer, reflection, personal relationships, and professional supervision, is not merely advisable but essential for the chaplains' well-being and the long-term sustainability of their ministry. The capacity for ethical decision-making is significantly impaired when a chaplain is overwhelmed or suffering from burnout.

The Bahamian context adds further layers of ethical complexity. The country's history of colonialism, its diverse religious landscape, and its complex social fabric all contribute to the unique ethical challenges faced by political chaplains. Navigating these complexities requires cultural sensitivity, a commitment to social justice, and a deep understanding of the power dynamics within Bahamian society. The political chaplain's role transcends partisan politics; it involves promoting reconciliation, fostering social harmony, and advocating for the well-being of all citizens, regardless of their political affiliation.

Ethical decision-making for a political chaplain isn't a matter of adhering to a simple checklist but requires constant self-reflection, careful discernment, and a willingness to engage in rigorous ethical deliberation. This process should ideally involve seeking guidance from mentors, colleagues, and relevant ethical frameworks, as well as from spiritual advisors. It's a continuous process of learning, growing, and refining one's approach to ethical dilemmas within the intricate tapestry of political life in The Bahamas. The goal is to serve both the political entity and the broader community with integrity, compassion, and unwavering commitment to the common good. This delicate balance demands sustained commitment and ongoing ethical reflection. The journey of a political chaplain is one of constant learning, adaptation, and a profound commitment to upholding the highest ethical standards.

REFLECTION STEP

While finishing this chapter, I attended a meeting at the Billy Graham Evangelistic Association in North Carolina. My friend, Rev. Ken Dunlap, shared a devotion from John 3:30 titled "He Must Increase, and I Must Decrease." When Heaven is present, Earth must take a back seat. Can you recall a time when you had to follow Heaven's way as a political chaplain? Share the outcome below.

____

____

____

____

____

____

____

____

____

____

____

____

____

____

REFLECTION (CONTINUED)

CHAPTER 5
Building Relationships and Networking within the Political Sphere

Building effective relationships within the Bahamian political landscape is paramount for a political chaplain. Unlike a traditional pastor whose sphere of influence is primarily defined by their congregation, the political chaplain navigates a far more intricate network of individuals with varying levels of power, influence, and often, conflicting agendas.

Success in this role hinges on the ability to cultivate trust, foster open communication, and navigate conflicts with grace and diplomacy. This requires a sophisticated understanding of the Bahamian political culture, its nuanced power dynamics, and the personalities who shape its trajectory.

Effective communication is the cornerstone of any successful relationship, particularly within the often-charged environment of Bahamian politics. This means more than simply conveying information; it involves active listening, empathy, and a genuine desire to understand opposing viewpoints. The political chaplain must be a skilled listener, capable of discerning the underlying concerns and anxieties of individuals, regardless of their political affiliation. This requires patience, a willingness to set aside personal biases, and a genuine respect for the dignity of every person encountered.

In the Bahamian context, where personal relationships often play a significant role in political decision-making, the ability to build rapport is crucial. This involves engaging with individuals on a personal level, showing genuine interest in their lives and concerns beyond their political roles. Building trust is a gradual process, earned through consistent reliability, integrity, and a demonstrated commitment to impartiality. It requires walking the tightrope between maintaining confidentiality and building trust, often a delicate balancing act in a world where information is a potent currency. Collaboration, rather than confrontation, is often the most effective approach to achieving positive outcomes in the political realm. This requires a willingness to find common ground, even on seemingly intractable issues. The political chaplain can act as a facilitator, bringing together diverse political actors to engage in constructive dialogue and explore mutually beneficial solutions. This role requires not only exceptional communication skills but also a deep understanding of the interests and motivations of the individuals involved. It's about understanding the unique history and social dynamics of the Bahamian political landscape and recognizing the influence of historical events and ingrained cultural norms. Success in this endeavor isn't just about building relationships, it's about understanding how those relationships fit into a larger, complex web of interconnected interests.

Conflict resolution is an unavoidable aspect of political life, and the political chaplain must be equipped with the skills to navigate these challenges effectively. This goes beyond simple mediation; it requires a deep understanding of the underlying causes of conflict, the emotional needs of those involved, and the broader political context in which the conflict arises. It's often about understanding unspoken grievances and addressing them in a way that respects the sensitivities involved. In the Bahamian context, this might involve navigating intricate family or community ties that influence political alliances and rivalries.

Networking is crucial for a political chaplain, allowing for the establishment of relationships across the political spectrum. This requires attending relevant events, engaging in meaningful

conversations, and cultivating relationships with individuals across different parties and factions. This isn't simply about collecting contacts; it's about building genuine relationships based on mutual respect and understanding. The ability to move between different political circles and maintain credibility and trust across the board is essential. Attending town halls, community events, and even informal gatherings provides valuable opportunities for building connections and understanding the concerns of various segments of the population.

Serving diverse constituencies is an essential aspect of the political chaplain's role. This involves being sensitive to the needs and concerns of people from different backgrounds, religions, and social groups. It requires going beyond simply acknowledging diversity; it means actively seeking out and engaging with marginalized communities, understanding their unique challenges, and advocating for their needs. This is particularly crucial in The Bahamas, with its rich multicultural fabric. The chaplain must demonstrate an understanding of the diverse cultural and religious contexts, ensuring an approach that is sensitive and inclusive.

The strategies for building relationships will vary depending on the individual and the context. For example, when engaging with a powerful political figure, a formal and respectful approach might be appropriate. However, when interacting with members of a grassroots organization, a more informal and participatory approach might be more effective. Flexibility and adaptability are essential traits for a successful political chaplain. Being able to adjust one's approach to meet the specific needs and preferences of each individual is crucial. It's not about applying a one-size-fits-all approach; it's about understanding the nuances of each interaction.

Building trust in a politically charged environment requires consistency and integrity. This involves keeping promises, being transparent in dealings, and consistently upholding ethical standards. Any breach of trust can have far-reaching consequences, severely undermining the chaplain's credibility and effectiveness.

Maintaining confidentiality is also paramount, particularly when dealing with sensitive personal information. The chaplain must create a safe space for individuals to share their concerns without fear of judgment or betrayal. This is especially critical when dealing with issues of a deeply personal or emotionally charged nature.

Furthermore, the political chaplain must be prepared to deal with setbacks and disappointments. Not every attempt to build a relationship will be successful, and not every conflict can be resolved. Resilience, perseverance, and a belief in the power of dialogue are crucial for navigating the inevitable challenges of working in a politically charged environment. This means learning from mistakes, adapting strategies, and continuing to strive for positive outcomes. There will be instances where bridges can't be built, or where attempts at mediation fail. The ability to accept these setbacks without losing hope or compromising one's ethical standards is a vital component of success.

The ethical considerations discussed earlier remain paramount. Building relationships should never come at the expense of integrity or impartiality. The political chaplain must always maintain a commitment to serving the broader community, not just a specific political party or faction. This includes avoiding favoritism, resisting undue influence, and using resources responsibly and equitably. Regular self-reflection, accountability mechanisms, and seeking advice from mentors or supervisors are vital for maintaining ethical standards in the often-challenging world of Bahamian politics. The potential for conflicts of interest remains a constant concern; the chaplain must maintain vigilance and adhere strictly to ethical guidelines.

The role of the political chaplain in The Bahamas is unique and demanding. Success in this vocation requires a sophisticated blend of pastoral skills, political acumen, and a deep commitment to ethical principles. The ability to build strong, trusting relationships across the political spectrum is crucial for effectively serving both the political entity and the wider community. It's a continuous process of learning, adapting, and striving to create a more harmonious and just society. By fostering understanding, promoting dialogue, and advocating for the common good, the political chaplain can play a vital role in shaping the political landscape of The Bahamas. The focus must remain on ethical conduct, transparent action, and a steadfast commitment to serving all, irrespective of political affiliation. This requires constant vigilance, self-reflection, and a deep commitment to the principles of fairness and justice. Ultimately, it's about using one's position to build bridges and foster a more unified and equitable society.

REFLECTION STEP

Relationships: *Relation* involve shared interests, while *ships* take you places. Identify some navigational goals for the political chaplain.

REFLECTION (CONTINUED)

CHAPTER 6
Providing Pastoral Care to Politicians and Staff

Providing pastoral care to politicians and their staff demands a nuanced understanding of the unique pressures inherent in the political arena. Unlike many professions, the intense scrutiny, public pressure, and often-vicious partisan battles can take a significant toll on mental and emotional well-being. Constant media attention, the need to maintain a public persona, and the relentless demands of campaigning and governance create an environment ripe for burnout, anxiety, and depression. The political chaplain, therefore, needs more than just theological training; they require a deep understanding of psychology, conflict resolution, and the specific stressors faced by those in public life.

One of the key challenges is building trust.

Politicians, by the nature of their work, are often wary of those they perceive as potential adversaries or sources of leaked information. This necessitates a deliberate and patient approach to relationship-building, emphasizing confidentiality and a non-judgmental stance. Active listening is paramount, allowing the individual to feel heard and understood without feeling judged or exploited. The chaplain must create a safe space where vulnerabilities can be shared without fear of reprisal or political manipulation. This requires more than just empathy; it demands the ability to discern underlying anxieties, unspoken fears, and the often-masked emotional toll of political life.

The pressure to maintain a carefully crafted public image can lead to a deep sense of isolation. Politicians often find themselves unable to share their struggles with friends and family, fearing the impact on their careers or public perception. The political chaplain can provide a much-needed outlet, a space where genuine emotions can be expressed without the filter of political strategy or public relations. This might involve helping them process criticism, navigate difficult relationships with colleagues or opponents, or simply providing a listening ear during times of intense stress. Counseling techniques in this context must be tailored to the individual's personality and the specific pressures they face.

Cognitive Behavioral Therapy (CBT) can be helpful in addressing anxiety and stress-related issues. It can equip politicians with practical strategies for managing overwhelming emotions, challenging negative thought patterns, and developing healthier coping mechanisms. Mindfulness techniques, such as meditation or deep breathing exercises, can also be incredibly beneficial in helping individuals manage stress and cultivate a sense of inner calm amidst the chaos of political life. However, it's crucial to remember that the chaplain's role isn't to provide therapy in the clinical sense; it's to offer pastoral support, often in conjunction with professional mental health practitioners.

Crisis intervention is another vital aspect of pastoral care for politicians and their staff. Unexpected events, such as election losses, public scandals, or personal tragedies, can trigger severe emotional distress. The chaplain must be prepared to respond swiftly and effectively, offering immediate support and guidance during these critical moments. This may involve connecting the individual with appropriate mental health professionals, providing practical assistance, or simply offering a reassuring presence during times of intense grief or uncertainty. The ability to mobilize a support network, including family, friends, and other trusted individuals, is crucial in mitigating the impact of crisis situations.

The pressures extend beyond the individual to their families and staff. Political life can strain family relationships, creating friction and resentment due to long hours, travel demands, and the constant presence of public scrutiny. The chaplain can provide support not only to the politician but also to their family members, helping them navigate the unique challenges of living in the public eye. Similarly, staff members often experience high levels of stress and pressure, working long hours under intense pressure. The chaplain can offer support and resources to staff, creating a culture of care and well-being within the political environment. This might involve organizing group sessions for stress management, facilitating team-building activities, or simply being a source of encouragement and support.

Effective pastoral care in a political context requires a keen awareness of ethical considerations. Confidentiality is paramount, and the chaplain must be scrupulous in protecting the privacy of those they serve. Avoiding any appearance of bias or favoritism is crucial, ensuring that pastoral support is offered equally to all members of the political team, regardless of their position or political views. The chaplain's role is not to offer political advice or engage in partisan politics, but rather to provide pastoral guidance and support to individuals regardless of their political beliefs.

Maintaining strict boundaries is essential to prevent any potential conflict of interest or compromise of professional integrity. This includes recognizing the limitations of one's expertise and referring individuals to appropriate professional services when necessary.

The provision of pastoral care to politicians and their staff requires a unique blend of pastoral skills, psychological insight, and a deep understanding of the political landscape. It's not a one-size-fits-all approach; the chaplain must adapt their strategies to meet the specific needs and circumstances of each individual. This involves being a skilled listener, a compassionate guide, and a steadfast source of support in the midst of immense pressure. By providing a safe space for vulnerability, offering practical coping mechanisms, and facilitating access to professional help when needed, the chaplain can play a crucial role in fostering the well-being of those who serve in the often-turbulent world of politics. The ongoing commitment to ethical conduct, continuous professional development, and self-care is essential for maintaining effectiveness and prevent burnout. The goal is not simply to manage stress, but to cultivate resilience, promote emotional well-being, and help individuals thrive, even amidst the relentless demands of political life. This approach cultivates a healthier political ecosystem, allowing for more effective leadership, improved policy outcomes, and a more harmonious society overall. The long-term benefits affect both the individuals served and the overall political process.

REFLECTION STEP

Please identify specific areas where improvement is needed in delivering pastoral care.

____

____

____

____

____

____

____

____

____

CHAPTER 7
Supporting First Responders in Crisis Situations

First responders—encompassing defence force, police, corrections, firefighters, paramedics, emergency medical technicians, and customs and immigration personnel—operate within a high-pressure environment characterized by constant exposure to trauma, violence, and death. The cumulative effect of witnessing suffering, responding to emergencies, and confronting life-threatening situations can have a profound and lasting impact on their mental and emotional well-being. Political chaplains, with their unique blend of pastoral care and community engagement, are uniquely positioned to offer critical support to this often-overlooked population. The chaplains' role extends beyond spiritual guidance; it encompasses practical assistance, emotional support, and fostering a sense of community and resilience.

Unlike politicians, whose challenges are often centered around public image and policy debates, first responders grapple with the immediate, visceral realities of human suffering. They bear witness to accidents, crimes, and natural disasters, often dealing with the aftermath of intense violence and unimaginable loss. This constant exposure to trauma can lead to a range of psychological and emotional issues, including Post-Traumatic Stress Disorder/Injury (PTSD/PTSI), depression, anxiety, substance abuse, and marital or family difficulties. The unique nature of their work also fosters a culture of stoicism and self-reliance, often hindering their ability to seek help when needed. They might internalize their emotional distress, believing that showing weakness is incompatible with their professional roles. This inherent reluctance to seek assistance makes the role of the political chaplain even more critical.

The political chaplain's approach to supporting first responders necessitates a deep understanding of the specific stressors inherent in their profession. This requires empathy, active listening skills, and a genuine appreciation for the sacrifices they make daily. A key aspect of this support is fostering a sense of trust and safety. First responders often operate in a culture of camaraderie and mutual respect, but they may be hesitant to confide in individuals outside their immediate professional circle. The chaplain needs to cultivate an environment where vulnerability is not seen as a sign of weakness but rather as an opportunity for healing and growth. This may involve establishing informal channels of communication, attending departmental events, or engaging in community outreach initiatives that demonstrate a genuine commitment to supporting their well-being.

Practical assistance can also form a vital part of the chaplain's support. This might involve connecting first responders with resources such as mental health professionals, substance abuse treatment programs, or financial aid if they are facing hardship. The chaplain can act as a liaison, navigating the bureaucratic complexities of these systems and advocating for the needs of the first responder. This practical support can be particularly crucial in the aftermath of traumatic events, when the individual might be overwhelmed by grief, anxiety, or the practical challenges of dealing with the immediate consequences of a crisis. This practical approach underscores that the support offered isn't merely spiritual or emotional, but also tangible and relevant to the everyday challenges faced by first responders.

Pastoral care for first responders extends beyond individual counseling and practical assistance. It often involves group support and community building. Group therapy sessions, facilitated by trained professionals or guided by the chaplain, can provide a safe space for first responders to share their experiences and connect with others who understand their challenges. These sessions provide a crucial opportunity to foster a sense of shared experience, reducing the feelings of isolation and stigma that often accompany trauma. Team-building activities and departmental events, attended by the chaplain, can help cultivate a supportive team environment within the first responder unit. By actively participating in their professional community, the chaplain becomes a trusted presence, demonstrating genuine care and understanding.

The chaplain's role also extends to working with the families of first responders. The constant stress and exposure to trauma can strain relationships, leading to marital problems, family conflict, and difficulties in parenting. The chaplain can offer individual and family counseling, mediating disputes, and helping family members cope with the emotional toll on their loved ones. This support network acknowledges that the impact of a first responder's work extends beyond the individual, influencing the well-being of their entire family unit. Therefore, a comprehensive approach to pastoral care involves working with the entire system of support around the first responder, recognizing that their well-being is inextricably linked to the health of their family and community.

One critical aspect often overlooked is the significance of addressing the ethical dilemmas that may arise. First responders sometimes encounter morally challenging situations that require profound ethical reflection. The chaplain can offer guidance and support in processing these experiences, helping them reconcile their actions with their personal values. These discussions can help prevent moral injury, a type of trauma resulting from moral conflict or transgression, which can be as debilitating as other forms of trauma. The chaplain's role is to facilitate ethical discernment, helping the first responder grapple with the complex moral dimensions of their work, and provide a non-judgmental space for introspection and reflection.

In addition to supporting first responders in the immediate aftermath of crises, the chaplain plays a vital role in preventing burnout and promoting long-term mental well-being. This involves establishing preventative measures, such as regular stress management workshops, mindfulness training, and encouraging healthy coping mechanisms. The chaplain can advocate for organizational changes that prioritize the mental health of first responders, such as improved access to mental health services, enhanced training in trauma management, and creating a more supportive work environment. This holistic approach focuses on proactive measures to build resilience, creating a culture that values and supports the mental health of first responders.

Furthermore, the political chaplain's engagement extends to advocating for policy changes that benefit first responders. This might involve working with lawmakers and policymakers to improve access to mental health care, increase funding for first responder support programs, and enact legislation that protects the rights and well-being of first responders. This advocacy aspect demonstrates a commitment to supporting not only individual first responders but also the wider system that shapes their work environment. By engaging in political advocacy, the chaplain actively contributes to creating a more supportive and sustainable system of care for this critical population.

Finally, the political chaplain must prioritize their own self-care. The demanding nature of this role, involving constant exposure to trauma and the emotional weight of supporting others, necessitates vigilance in maintaining their own mental and emotional well-being. Regular self-reflection, peer support groups, and professional supervision are vital in preventing compassion fatigue and burnout.

This self-awareness is crucial, not only for the chaplain's personal well-being, but also in preserving effectiveness in providing support to others. A burnt-out chaplain is unable to effectively support those in

need. Therefore, a commitment to personal well-being is an integral aspect of fulfilling this vital role. The political chaplain, through compassionate support and proactive engagement, acts as a vital link between first responders and the larger community, fostering both individual resilience and systemic change that prioritizes the well-being of those who risk their lives to protect others.

REFLECTION STEP

Can you suggest an initiative to support first responders in your community? Please share your idea here.

____

____

____

____

____

____

____

____

____

____

____

____

REFLECTION (CONTINUED)

CHAPTER 8
Community Engagement and Outreach Programs

The effectiveness of a political chaplain extends far beyond the individual support offered to first responders. Their role significantly impacts community well-being through strategic engagement and outreach programs. These initiatives are crucial not only for building stronger communities but also for fostering a sense of shared responsibility and collective resilience, particularly in the face of adversity. A chaplain's engagement transcends partisan politics; it focuses on the shared humanity that binds a community together, promoting social cohesion and addressing underlying societal challenges.

One powerful aspect of community engagement involves establishing meaningful partnerships with local organizations. This collaborative approach amplifies the chaplain's impact, allowing for a more comprehensive and effective response to community needs. For instance, collaborating with local charities can provide essential resources such as food banks, clothing drives, and housing assistance to those facing hardship. Partnerships with mental health organizations broaden access to counseling and support services, extending the reach of mental health initiatives to those who might otherwise be unable to access them. Collaborating with schools can lead to youth mentoring programs, providing guidance and support to at-risk youth, strengthening community bonds, and promoting a culture of civic engagement. By working alongside other community leaders, such as social workers, educators, and community activists, the chaplain builds a network of support that addresses a broader spectrum of community needs.

Building trust and rapport within the community is paramount. This requires consistent presence, active listening, and a genuine commitment to understanding the unique challenges faced by various segments of the population. This isn't simply about attending community events; it's about fostering genuine relationships based on mutual respect and empathy. Regular visits to community outreaches, hospitals, and senior citizen homes demonstrate a tangible commitment to being present and available to those in need. Participating in community dialogues and forums provides a platform for listening to community concerns, fostering open communication, and promoting a sense of inclusivity. The chaplain's role as a trusted confidant allows them to be a bridge between diverse groups, mediating conflicts, and fostering understanding.

Effective community outreach often involves identifying and addressing specific needs within the community. This might involve conducting needs assessments to pinpoint the areas requiring immediate attention. For instance, research might reveal high rates of unemployment, poverty, or substance abuse, guiding the chaplain towards targeted initiatives. Such research provides a framework for developing tailored programs that address the identified issues. For example, if unemployment is prevalent, the chaplain might work with local businesses to develop job training programs or connect unemployed individuals with employment agencies. If substance abuse is a significant problem, the chaplain could collaborate with treatment centers to provide access to addiction services and support groups. By addressing specific needs, the chaplain demonstrates a practical commitment to improving the lives of community members.

Furthermore, community outreach programs can take many forms, extending beyond direct services. For example, organizing community events such as sports days, family picnics, and holiday celebrations fosters a sense of belonging and creates opportunities for social interaction. These events can build relationships and a sense of collective identity within the community, counteracting feelings of isolation. Similarly, initiating literacy programs, offering after-school activities, or providing access to recreational facilities promotes the well-being of young people, empowering them and creating a pathway for future success. These initiatives not only meet immediate needs but also lay a foundation for a stronger and more vibrant community in the long term.

The political chaplain's role often involves addressing social justice issues that impact the community. This might involve advocating for policies that promote equality, combat discrimination, and ensure access to essential services. For example, the chaplain might advocate affordable housing initiatives, access to quality healthcare, or fair wages for workers. This advocacy can extend to raising awareness about social justice issues, promoting dialogue, and mobilizing community members to take collective action. The chaplains' position allows them to act as a voice for the marginalized, amplifying their concerns and promoting social change. Through public speaking engagements, community workshops, and partnerships with advocacy groups, chaplains can mobilize support for positive social change.

One particularly crucial role of the political chaplain is mediation and conflict resolution. Communities often grapple with internal conflicts stemming from differing viewpoints, socioeconomic disparities, or historical grievances. The chaplain's neutral position and commitment to pastoral care makes them uniquely positioned to facilitate dialogue, build bridges, and promote reconciliation.

Their mediation efforts may involve bringing conflicting parties together, helping them understand each other's perspectives, and facilitating a peaceful resolution. This restorative approach strengthens the social fabric of the community and promotes long-term harmony.

Moreover, the political chaplain can play a pivotal role in crisis response. In the event of natural disasters, community tragedies, or other crises, the chaplain offers crucial support to those affected. This might involve providing immediate assistance, coordinating relief efforts, and offering spiritual and emotional support to those grappling with grief and loss. Their presence during times of crisis provides a source of comfort, hope, and stability, helping the community navigate difficult times. Following such events, the chaplain can play a vital role in the rebuilding process, facilitating community healing and recovery.

Crucially, the success of any community engagement program hinges on effective evaluation and adaptation. This requires regularly assessing the impact of initiatives and making necessary adjustments to optimize their effectiveness. This might involve tracking key indicators such as participation rates, community feedback, and the achievement of program goals. The data collected informs future program design, ensuring that resources are allocated effectively and that community needs are adequately addressed. Flexibility and responsiveness to evolving community needs is essential to ensure the long-term success of these endeavors. Continuous evaluation also facilitates accountability and demonstrates a commitment to transparency and responsibility to the community.

Finally, the role of the political chaplain in community engagement and outreach is not without its challenges. Navigating the complexities of political affiliations, diverse viewpoints, and potentially contentious issues require sensitivity, tact, and a commitment to impartiality. Maintaining a delicate balance between political involvement and community service is essential.

The chaplain's primary focus remains serving the community's needs, irrespective of political affiliations. This requires strong ethical decision-making, transparency in actions, and a deep commitment to serving the common good. By diligently addressing these challenges, the political chaplain reinforces their credibility and strengthens their role as a trusted leader and advocate within the community. The political chaplain, through dedicated community engagement, acts as a vital force for positive change, fostering resilience, promoting social justice, and strengthening the bonds that unite a community.

REFLECTION STEP

Evaluate the community and identify the programs with which you wish to establish connections, providing a rationale for each selection.

REFLECTION (CONTINUED)

REFLECTION (CONTINUED)

CHAPTER 9

Developing and Implementing Effective Communication Strategies

Effective communication is the bedrock of successful political chaplaincy. It's the bridge that connects chaplains to the individuals, groups, and communities they serve, fostering trust, understanding, and ultimately, positive change. Without clear, compassionate, and strategically deployed communication, even the most well-intentioned initiatives will struggle to achieve their intended impact. This requires a multi-faceted approach, encompassing clear messaging, active listening, conflict resolution techniques, and a savvy understanding of media engagement.

First, let's consider the importance of clear and compassionate communication. This involves articulating messages in a way that is easily understood by the target audience, regardless of their background or level of political engagement. It means avoiding jargon, complex terminology, and overly formal language that can alienate or confuse. Instead, opting for straightforward, accessible language ensures that the message resonates with the intended recipient. Equally crucial is the compassionate delivery of the message. This involves conveying empathy, understanding, and a genuine concern for the well-being of others. This is especially important when addressing sensitive topics, such as grief, loss, trauma, or social injustice. A chaplain's communication style should reflect their deep-seated care and genuine desire to support those they serve. This sensitivity and understanding cultivate trust, creating a space where individuals feel safe and comfortable sharing their thoughts and feelings. Consider, for instance, communicating with a family who has lost a loved one in a politically motivated attack. A clear, concise explanation of the services available, delivered with empathy and respect, can be far more effective than a formal, impersonal announcement.

Secondly, effective communication in political chaplaincy necessitates mastery of conflict resolution. Political environments are inherently prone to disagreements, tensions, and even outright conflict. Chaplains, in their unique role, must be adept at mediating disputes, facilitating dialogue, and promoting understanding between differing perspectives. This often involves active listening, demonstrating empathy for all involved parties, and helping them identify common ground. It's not about taking sides, but rather about fostering a safe space where all voices can be heard and respected. Consider a scenario where opposing political factions are embroiled in a bitter feud within a community. The chaplain, through patient mediation and careful communication, can facilitate discussions, identify the root causes of the conflict, and help the parties develop a mutually acceptable solution. This might involve brainstorming collaborative projects, focusing on shared goals, or implementing mechanisms for peaceful conflict resolution in the future. The chaplain's role is not to judge or impose a solution, but to guide the process, ensuring that all parties feel heard and respected, contributing to the healing and reconciliation of the community.

Thirdly, media engagement plays a significant role in the outreach and impact of a political chaplain. In today's interconnected world, the ability to effectively communicate through various media platforms is essential. This involves understanding the nuances of different media, tailoring messages accordingly, and utilizing these platforms to amplify the chaplain's message and reach a wider audience. This could involve preparing press releases, giving interviews to local news outlets, or utilizing social media platforms to engage with the community. However, it's crucial to approach media engagement with a clear understanding of the ethical considerations

involved. Maintaining objectivity and avoiding partisan bias are critical, ensuring that the chaplain's message remains focused on community well-being and social harmony, rather than promoting any specific political agenda. For example, after a national tragedy, a chaplain may use a television interview to offer comfort and guidance to the grieving nation, while also highlighting resources and support available to those affected. The skill lies in utilizing media platforms to spread a message of hope and unity without becoming embroiled in contentious political debate.

Tailoring communication to diverse audiences is another critical aspect of effective communication strategies for political chaplains. Communities are comprised of people from diverse backgrounds, experiences, and belief systems. Effective communication necessitates adapting one's approach to effectively reach each segment of the community. This requires sensitivity and an understanding of cultural nuances, linguistic differences, and varying levels of political engagement. A chaplain must be able to communicate complex information in a way that is accessible and understandable to individuals with varying levels of education and literacy. For example, explaining the government's response to a crisis requires different approaches depending on whether the audience consists of highly educated professionals, community leaders, or less informed members of the public. Chaplains must adopt flexible communication strategies, tailoring their style to suit the specific audience and ensuring that the message resonates with everyone.

Moreover, navigating sensitive political situations requires careful consideration and a high degree of emotional intelligence. Chaplains often find themselves dealing with situations that are highly charged and emotionally fraught, involving issues of intense political debate and potentially conflicting viewpoints. Effective communication in such situations demands sensitivity, tact, and the ability to maintain neutrality. It is important to be prepared to respond to challenging questions, accusations, or critiques with grace and professionalism. The goal is not to win an argument or score a political point, but to foster dialogue and reconciliation. For instance, in a post-election period of heightened tension, the chaplain might engage in community forums to address concerns, build bridges between opposing groups, and promote healing and reconciliation. This demands tact and emotional intelligence, ensuring the conversations are focused on collaboration and mutual understanding, rather than descending into unproductive arguments or accusations.

Finally, technology plays an increasingly important role in enhancing communication outreach. Utilizing various technological tools can significantly expand the reach of the chaplain's message, allowing them to connect with individuals and communities more effectively. This includes utilizing social media platforms, creating online resources, and employing email communication to reach a wider audience. However, the use of technology should be balanced with traditional communication methods, maintaining personal connections and fostering face-to-face interactions. It is important to ensure that technology enhances, rather than replaces, the chaplain's ability to build genuine relationships and foster empathy. For instance, a chaplain may utilize a website or social media page to provide updates on community programs, share inspirational messages, or offer online resources for emotional support and counseling. But such digital engagement should complement, not supplant, the crucial human interactions that are at the heart of effective pastoral care and community service. The key is to integrate technology strategically, creating a holistic and effective communication approach that allows the chaplain to reach and serve a wider audience. In essence, the effective political chaplain leverages a wide array of communication tools to accomplish the goal: building community bridges, fostering empathy, and

promoting understanding. Through carefully calibrated messaging, proactive conflict resolution, and savvy media engagement, political chaplains strengthen their role as trusted leaders, committed to the well-being of all within their political landscape.

REFLECTION STEP

The Nassau Guardian and *The Tribune News Outlets* have extended an offer for you to write a daily column. They have requested that you provide a title for your column as well as an explanation for your choice. What would your column be titled, and what is the reasoning behind this selection?

REFLECTION (CONTINUED)

CHAPTER 10
Resource Management and Collaboration with Other Agencies

Resource management is a critical skill for political chaplains, demanding careful planning, strategic partnerships, and a keen eye for both immediate needs and long-term sustainability. Securing adequate funding is paramount, as it underpins the chaplain's ability to provide essential services and programs. This isn't simply a matter of applying for grants; it necessitates building a comprehensive fundraising strategy that leverages diverse avenues.

One such avenue is cultivating relationships with philanthropic organizations, foundations, and individual donors who align with the chaplain's mission and values. This requires presenting a compelling narrative that clearly articulates the impact of the chaplain's work on the community, demonstrating both the immediate needs being addressed and the long-term positive outcomes that are envisioned. Compelling proposals should articulate clear, measurable goals, offering specific examples of the services provided and the measurable impact achieved. This data-driven approach ensures accountability and reinforces the value of the chaplain's work to potential funders.

Furthermore, exploring government funding opportunities, both at the local and national level, is essential. This requires understanding the relevant grant programs and their eligibility criteria, crafting proposals that meet those criteria, and building relationships with government officials who can champion the chaplain's applications. Networking with other organizations, both within the political sphere and the broader community, also presents vital opportunities for securing funding. Collaborative projects jointly submitted grant applications, and shared resources can significantly enhance the chaplain's funding capacity. A successful strategy will involve not only seeking funding but also actively managing the finances with transparency and accountability. This includes maintaining accurate financial records, adhering to strict budgeting guidelines, and producing regular financial reports for funders and stakeholders. Transparency fosters trust and demonstrates responsible stewardship of the resources entrusted to the chaplain. Beyond funding, resource management encompasses building strategic partnerships with other agencies and organizations.

Effective collaboration is essential for optimizing resource utilization and ensuring comprehensive service delivery. This includes forging alliances with law enforcement agencies, social services organizations, healthcare providers, and community groups. For example, collaborating with local law enforcement can provide insights into community needs and facilitate access to individuals who may require pastoral care or support. Working with social service agencies can help connect individuals with relevant resources, such as housing assistance, food banks, or job training programs. Similarly, partnerships with healthcare providers can facilitate access to mental health services and other forms of medical care, while collaboration with community groups can expand the chaplain's reach and impact within specific neighborhoods or demographic groups.

These collaborations must be structured strategically. They necessitate clear communication, shared goals, and a well-defined framework for cooperation. This might involve formal agreements, memoranda of understanding, or regular meetings to coordinate activities and share information. Regular communication channels will help ensure that all parties involved are informed about program developments and any emerging challenges. The key is to foster an environment of mutual respect and shared responsibility, valuing the expertise and perspectives of all participating organizations. This collaborative model enhances the effectiveness of the chaplain's work, ensuring that individuals receive a comprehensive and integrated range of support services.

Furthermore, accessing support services for oneself is crucial for the sustainability of the chaplain's ministry. The demanding nature of political chaplaincy can exact a toll on the individual, and access to appropriate support services is not a sign of weakness, but rather a sign of professional responsibility. Political chaplains should actively pursue professional supervision, peer support groups, and mental health services to maintain their well-being and prevent burnout. Recognizing the unique stressors inherent in this role is critical. These might include exposure to traumatic events, constant demands on time and emotional energy, and the potential for conflict or polarization within the political arena. Addressing these stressors proactively helps prevent emotional exhaustion and maintain the chaplain's capacity for effective service. Establishing a strong support network is vital—this could include other chaplains, mentors, and trusted friends or family members. These individuals can offer emotional support, guidance, and a sense of community, helping to mitigate the challenges of the role.

Effective resource management extends to program evaluation. To ensure accountability and continuous improvement, political chaplains should develop a system for evaluating the effectiveness of their programs and services. This requires setting measurable goals and objectives, collecting data on program outcomes, and analyzing that data to assess progress and identify areas for improvement. Methods of evaluation could include surveys, interviews, focus groups, and analysis of program records. This data-driven approach demonstrates the impact of the chaplain's work, supporting the case for continued funding and demonstrating the value of their ministry. This process should be transparent and accountable, involving stakeholders from different sectors, fostering a spirit of collaborative evaluation and improvement. Regular review of program effectiveness ensures that resources are allocated efficiently and that services are tailored to meet the evolving needs of the community.

Finally, a crucial element of resource management in political chaplaincy is conflict resolution. Political environments are inherently conflictual, and chaplains might find themselves mediating disputes or navigating sensitive situations. Effective conflict management is essential, not only for maintaining peaceful relations within the political arena but also for the chaplain's own well-being. This requires developing strong conflict resolution skills, including active listening, empathy, and the ability to facilitate dialogue between opposing factions. It's vital to remain neutral and impartial, fostering an environment where all parties feel heard and respected. Focusing on shared goals and identifying common ground can help de-escalate tensions and build bridges between differing viewpoints. The chaplain's role is to promote understanding and reconciliation, not to take sides or impose solutions. This capacity to de-escalate and navigate disagreements is not only essential for the smooth functioning of the political environment but also contributes to the chaplain's personal well-being by mitigating the impact of conflict. This requires a proactive approach to conflict, developing preventative strategies and being prepared to engage in mediation when needed.

In conclusion, successful political chaplaincy demands a multifaceted approach to resource management. It involves securing diverse funding streams, building strategic partnerships, prioritizing access to personal support services, and implementing rigorous program evaluation. By effectively managing resources and collaborating with other agencies, political chaplains can optimize service delivery, enhance community well-being, and sustain their own ministry in the long term. The ability to navigate the complexities

of political life while maintaining a focus on pastoral care and community service is a testament to the adaptability and resilience of political chaplains, a vital component of a thriving and functional political landscape. The responsible and effective management of resources ensures not only the viability of the chaplain's work but also its positive impact on the broader community they serve.

REFLECTION STEP

If you were to assemble a management team, which three qualities would be most important to you, and why?

____

____

____

____

____

____

____

____

____

____

____

____

REFLECTION (CONTINUED)

58

CHAPTER 11

Recognizing and Managing Stress and Burnout

The demanding nature of political chaplaincy, interwoven with the complexities of the political landscape and the inherent emotional weight of pastoral care, presents unique challenges to well-being. Ignoring the potential for stress and burnout is not only detrimental to the chaplain's personal health but also compromises effectiveness in ministry. This section explores the common stressors faced by political chaplains, providing practical strategies for recognizing, managing, and preventing burnout, fostering resilience and sustained service.

One of the most significant stressors is the constant exposure to high-pressure situations. Political environments are often volatile, characterized by intense debates, power struggles, and sometimes, outright conflict. Chaplains may find themselves mediating disputes, offering comfort to individuals experiencing the emotional fallout of political decisions, or navigating ethical dilemmas related to political allegiance and community service. This consistent exposure to conflict and high stakes can lead to chronic stress, manifesting in both physical and psychological symptoms. Physical symptoms can range from fatigue and sleep disturbances to headaches, digestive problems, and weakened immunity. Psychologically, the chaplain may experience anxiety, irritability, difficulty concentrating, emotional exhaustion, and feelings of cynicism or detachment. Another significant stressor stems from the emotional demands of the role. Political chaplains often act as confidantes, providing support and guidance to individuals grappling with personal crises, grief, or moral challenges. These emotional burdens can accumulate over time, leading to compassion fatigue, a state of emotional and physical exhaustion caused by prolonged exposure to suffering. This fatigue isn't simply a matter of tiredness; it's a deeper exhaustion that can erode the chaplain's empathy and capacity for emotional connection.

The constant need to offer comfort and support, without adequate time for self-reflection or rejuvenation, contributes to this emotional depletion. Recognizing the signs of compassion fatigue is crucial. These signs may include feeling emotionally drained, having difficulty connecting with others, experiencing detachment or cynicism, or exhibiting a diminished sense of purpose in one's work.

Time constraints frequently exacerbate the stress experienced by political chaplains. The demands of the role often extend beyond the traditional working hours, requiring long hours, weekend work, and on-call availability. This can lead to a significant disruption in work and life balance, potentially affecting personal relationships and overall well-being. The pressure to meet multiple demands—pastoral care, administrative duties, community engagement, and relationship-building within the political sphere—can be overwhelming, leading to feelings of being stretched too thin. This constant pressure can impact sleep quality, family life, and personal time, contributing to chronic stress and potentially leading to burnout. Effective time management techniques, including prioritization, delegation, and setting realistic boundaries, are therefore essential for managing these pressures.

The ethical dilemmas inherent in political chaplaincy add another layer of complexity. Balancing political allegiance with the broader needs of the community often requires difficult choices, potentially placing the chaplain in uncomfortable or morally challenging situations. Maintaining impartiality while supporting individuals with diverse viewpoints, beliefs, and affiliations requires careful navigation and a strong ethical compass. The pressure to remain neutral, while simultaneously offering comfort and support to all parties, can lead to moral distress, a state of emotional distress resulting from a perceived violation of one's ethical principles. Regular reflection on one's ethical framework, seeking counsel from trusted mentors or colleagues, and engaging in continuing professional development can provide guidance and support in navigating these ethical complexities.

Recognizing and proactively managing stress is not merely an act of self-preservation; it's a professional imperative for political chaplains. The effectiveness of their ministry is intrinsically linked to their own well-being. Neglecting self-care compromises their ability to provide compassionate and effective support to others. Therefore, implementing strategies for stress reduction and prevention is crucial for sustaining their ministry in the long term.

Stress management techniques are essential tools for political chaplains. These techniques can range from simple relaxation exercises like deep breathing and progressive muscle relaxation to more structured approaches like mindfulness meditation. Deep breathing exercises, for instance, can calm the nervous system and reduce feelings of anxiety in stressful situations. Mindfulness practices, which involve paying attention to the present moment without judgment, can increase self-awareness and help to manage emotional reactivity. Regular physical exercise is also vital for stress reduction. Exercise not only releases endorphins, which have mood-boosting effects, but also improves sleep quality and overall physical health. It's important to find activities that are enjoyable and sustainable, whether it be running, swimming, or simply a daily walk.

Prioritizing sleep is another crucial aspect of self-care. Adequate sleep is essential for both physical and mental restoration. Lack of sleep impairs cognitive function, reduces emotional resilience, and increases susceptibility to stress. Establishing a regular sleep schedule, creating a relaxing bedtime routine, and ensuring a conducive sleep environment can contribute to improved sleep quality. These might involve limiting screen time before bed, practicing relaxation techniques, and creating a quiet, dark, and cool sleep space. Addressing sleep problems proactively, including seeking professional help if needed, is crucial.

Maintaining a healthy diet is also important. A balanced diet provides the essential nutrients needed for both physical and mental well-being. Focusing on nutrient-rich foods, while minimizing processed foods, sugary drinks, and excessive caffeine, can contribute to increased energy levels and improved mood. Hydration is equally crucial; staying properly hydrated can improve cognitive function and reduce fatigue.

Building and nurturing strong support networks is critical. Political chaplains should cultivate relationships with other chaplains, mentors, friends, and family members who can offer emotional support, understanding, and a sense of community. Sharing experiences and burdens with others who understand the unique challenges of the profession can significantly reduce feelings of isolation and improve emotional resilience. Seeking professional supervision or counseling is not a sign of weakness, but rather a testament to responsible professional practice. A therapist or counselor can provide a safe space for processing difficult emotions, gaining insights into personal coping strategies, and developing more effective stress management techniques.

Creating boundaries between work and personal life is essential for avoiding burnout. This might involve setting clear limitations on working hours, establishing designated time for personal activities and relationships, and actively disconnecting from work during non-working hours. This can be challenging in the demanding world of political chaplaincy, but it's a critical step in preventing burnout. Regular breaks throughout the day, even short ones, are also essential for maintaining focus and preventing emotional exhaustion. This could involve taking short walks, doing mindfulness exercises, or simply stepping away from one's workspace for a few minutes. Regular self-reflection and spiritual practices are equally crucial. This involves taking time for introspection, reviewing personal experiences, identifying areas for growth, and reaffirming one's sense of purpose. Engaging in spiritual practices, such as prayer, meditation, or spending time in nature, can provide solace, promote emotional regulation, and foster a sense of connection to something larger than oneself.

Finally, prioritizing personal hobbies and interests is vital for maintaining overall well-being. Engaging in activities that are enjoyable and provide a sense of relaxation and fulfillment contributes to a balanced life and helps to prevent burnout. This could involve spending time with loved ones, pursuing creative pursuits, reading, or engaging in any activity that brings joy and relaxation. Remember, self-care is not selfish; it's a necessary investment in maintaining one's effectiveness and resilience in the demanding field of political chaplaincy. By actively implementing these strategies, political chaplains can safeguard their well-being, ensuring they remain effective in their vital ministry and contribute significantly to the communities they serve.

REFECTION STEP

In relation to this chapter on Recognizing and Managing Stress and Burnout, please identify three to five modifications you need to implement.

CHAPTER 12
Maintaining Boundaries and Avoiding Compassion Fatigue

Maintaining healthy boundaries is paramount for political chaplains, not merely a suggestion for personal well-being but a crucial element of effective and sustainable ministry. The constant exposure to the emotional intensity of political life, coupled with the inherent demands of pastoral care, creates a fertile ground for compassion fatigue and burnout. Without a clear understanding of personal limits and the conscious effort to enforce them, chaplains risk becoming overwhelmed, depleted, and ultimately ineffective in their role.

Self-awareness forms the cornerstone of boundary setting. Before chaplains can effectively establish boundaries with others, they must first understand their own limits. This involves a process of honest self-reflection, perhaps facilitated through journaling, meditation, or conversations with trusted mentors. What are the chaplain's emotional thresholds? At what point do they feel overwhelmed, stressed, or depleted? Identifying these triggers is the first step toward preventing them from escalating into burnout. This self-assessment might reveal a pattern—perhaps prolonged exposure to conflict triggers anxiety, or an accumulation of emotionally charged conversations leads to exhaustion. Once these patterns are recognized, the chaplain can develop proactive strategies to mitigate their impact.

Self-compassion is inextricably linked to self-awareness. Recognizing personal limitations is not an admission of weakness but an act of self-preservation.

Chaplains who demand perfection from themselves, relentlessly pushing their boundaries, are especially vulnerable to burnout.

Cultivating self-compassion means acknowledging that it's acceptable to experience emotional exhaustion and to take steps to recover. It's a matter of recognizing that caring for others effectively begins with caring for oneself. This might involve forgiving oneself for imperfections or setting aside time for rest and rejuvenation without guilt. The concept of self-compassion involves treating oneself with the same kindness and understanding one would offer a friend facing similar challenges.

Establishing clear boundaries with politicians requires a delicate balance. While the chaplain's role may involve close collaboration and building trust, it's essential to define the limits of their availability and the nature of their involvement. This might involve setting specific times for meetings, limiting the frequency of phone calls outside working hours, and clearly articulating roles and responsibilities. It's crucial to avoid becoming overly involved in political strategies or internal party conflicts, maintaining a position of impartiality and focusing on providing pastoral support to individuals rather than becoming entangled in partisan disputes.

This boundary setting isn't about detachment; instead, it protects the integrity of the chaplain's role and prevents emotional over-investment in highly charged situations. Setting these limits might involve politely declining requests that fall outside the defined scope of duties or redirecting conversations that stray into potentially divisive political territory. Boundaries with community members are equally important, particularly when dealing with sensitive issues or personal crises.

While empathy and compassion are vital, the chaplain needs to establish clear limits to prevent emotional entanglement or the blurring of professional and personal relationships. This means carefully managing expectations, providing appropriate levels of support without becoming over-involved in individuals' lives, and recognizing the importance of maintaining professional distance.

It's vital to remember that chaplains are not therapists or counselors; their role is primarily pastoral, offering spiritual guidance and support rather than undertaking extended therapeutic interventions. Referring individuals to appropriate professional services when needed is not a failure but a demonstration of responsible professional conduct. This might involve connecting individuals with mental health professionals, social workers, or other community resources, ensuring they receive the specialized care they require.

Practical strategies for preventing emotional exhaustion often involve proactive self-care practices. These extend beyond the usual advice of sufficient sleep and balanced nutrition (although these remain essential). Consider techniques like time blocking: specifically allocating time for various tasks and activities, including periods of dedicated rest and relaxation. This structured approach can help prevent the chaotic accumulation of demands that frequently lead to overwhelm. Prioritizing tasks is also crucial. Learning to distinguish between urgent and important tasks allows for the more strategic allocation of energy and prevents the feeling of being constantly reactive.

Regular debriefing with colleagues or mentors provides a valuable mechanism for processing intense emotional experiences. A supportive peer group can act as a safe space to share experiences, receive emotional support, and gain fresh perspectives on challenging situations.

This shared understanding mitigates feelings of isolation and fosters a sense of community, reducing the burden of carrying emotional weight alone. Such discussions should focus on strategies for handling difficult situations, sharing successful techniques, and mutual support in navigating ethical dilemmas. Formal supervision can complement these peer-support networks, providing a structured opportunity for reflection and professional growth.

Spiritual practices provide another crucial layer of resilience for political chaplains. Engaging in prayer, meditation, or other contemplative practices can foster inner peace, replenish emotional reserves, and reinforce a sense of purpose. These practices are not simply for personal solace but can be vital for maintaining emotional equilibrium in demanding situations. Regular introspection, through prayer or journaling, enables the chaplain to critically reflect on their experiences, process emotions effectively, and maintain clarity and focus.

Regular breaks throughout the day, and extended periods of leave, are not luxuries but necessities. These breaks serve as crucial opportunities to disconnect from work, recharge emotional batteries, and prevent burnout. These may involve extended periods away from the office, or weekends specifically dedicated to personal interests and family time. Chaplains should explicitly schedule these periods of disengagement as part of their routine, rather than leaving them to chance. This requires a proactive and deliberate commitment to self-care and boundary setting.

In conclusion, maintaining boundaries and avoiding compassion fatigue requires a multifaceted approach encompassing self-awareness, self-compassion, proactive self-care, and the establishment of clear boundaries with both politicians and community members. By implementing these strategies, political chaplains can ensure their own well-being and maintain their effectiveness in their vital ministry, preventing emotional exhaustion and sustaining their service over the long term. The pursuit of these practices is not a sign of weakness but a crucial element of responsible professional conduct, necessary to effectively serve those within the often-turbulent waters of political life.

REFLECTION STEP

What boundaries have you established for yourself? Please share.

REFLECTION (CONTINUED)

CHAPTER 13

Building a Strong Support Network and Seeking Mentorship

Building a robust support network is not merely advantageous for political chaplains; it's essential for their survival and effectiveness.

The unique pressures of this role—balancing the demands of a political environment with the sensitive needs of individuals—demand a strong scaffolding of support. Without it, the risk of burnout, compassion fatigue, and ultimately, failure in ministry, becomes significantly heightened. This support system should be multifaceted, encompassing peer support, professional supervision, and mentorship from experienced individuals in similar or related fields.

Peer support provides an invaluable source of strength. Connecting with other political chaplains, or those working in similarly demanding roles within the public or social services sectors, creates a safe space to share experiences, frustrations, and successes. This sharing isn't just about venting; it's about gaining alternative perspectives, learning from the mistakes and triumphs of others, and feeling a sense of shared understanding that mitigates feelings of isolation. Finding these connections may involve attending professional conferences, joining relevant associations, or actively seeking out colleagues in similar roles within different political parties or organizations. Establishing regular meetings, either in-person or virtually, allows for the consistent exchange of support and the development of lasting professional bonds. These meetings could focus on case studies, ethical dilemmas, or simply sharing coping mechanisms for navigating the stressors inherent in the role.

The opportunity to witness how others successfully navigate challenging situations can significantly contribute to resilience and emotional well-being.

Beyond informal peer support, formal professional supervision offers a structured approach to professional development and self-reflection. Supervision sessions, ideally with an experienced clinical supervisor or a chaplaincy mentor, provide a confidential setting to explore complex cases, examine one's own emotional responses to challenging situations, and develop effective strategies for managing personal and professional boundaries. Supervision helps chaplains identify personal patterns of behavior, such as tendencies toward over-involvement or emotional exhaustion, and devise strategies for self-correction. It also provides a safe space to process difficult ethical dilemmas, ensuring the chaplain acts with integrity and aligns their actions with professional guidelines and their own conscience. In the uniquely challenging context of political chaplaincy, supervision is not a luxury but a necessary safeguard against potential ethical pitfalls and professional burnout. The clarity and objectivity provided by a supervisor can be invaluable in navigating the delicate balance between loyalty, impartiality, and pastoral care.

Mentorship provides a different, yet equally important, form of support. Mentors, ideally senior political chaplains or individuals with significant experience navigating the demands of public service, offer guidance based on their own accumulated wisdom.

They can act as role models, offering insights into effective strategies for boundary setting, conflict resolution, and maintaining personal well-being in the face of intense pressure. A mentor's role is not merely advisory; it's about fostering growth and providing encouragement through the challenges inherent in this specialized ministry. Finding a mentor may involve reaching out to respected figures within the field, attending workshops or conferences where potential mentors may be present, or seeking recommendations from trusted colleagues. The mentor-mentee relationship should be built on mutual respect and trust, with clear communication regarding expectations and boundaries. Regular meetings, perhaps quarterly or monthly, can be structured to discuss specific professional challenges, personal growth aspirations, and reflections on professional practice.

Spiritual direction offers a unique form of support tailored to the spiritual needs of the chaplain. In a role demanding constant engagement with the complex emotions and moral ambiguities of political life, maintaining a strong spiritual foundation is critical. A spiritual director, ideally someone with experience in pastoral counseling or spiritual guidance, provides a space for reflection on one's faith journey, prayer life, and overall sense of purpose. This support complements the professional aspects of supervision and mentorship, focusing on the spiritual and personal well-being of the chaplain. It provides a space for honest introspection, exploration of personal values, and discernment in the face of moral dilemmas. The spiritual director helps the chaplain integrate their faith with their professional life, ensuring their spiritual well-being remains strong amidst the potential pressures of political engagement.

Personal reflection, in addition to spiritual direction, plays a crucial role in sustaining resilience. Maintaining a reflective practice through journaling, meditation, or simply taking quiet time for contemplation allows chaplains to process daily experiences, identify patterns of stress, and evaluate their effectiveness in responding to challenges. Regular reflection isn't just about debriefing; it's about cultivating self-awareness, understanding one's emotional responses, and identifying strategies for self-care. This might involve setting aside time for quiet prayer, meditation, or simply engaging in activities that promote relaxation and emotional renewal.

The importance of setting aside time for personal reflection cannot be overstated. It's not a luxury; it's a crucial component of self-preservation. The demands of political chaplaincy are relentless; a failure to engage in regular self-reflection, self-care, and emotional processing will inevitably lead to depletion and burnout. The methods used for self-reflection are less critical than the consistent commitment to the practice itself. What matters is that the chaplain makes the time to disconnect, process their emotions, and recharge their emotional reserves.

Building these supportive relationships requires proactive engagement. Chaplains must actively seek out peers, mentors, and spiritual directors, establishing clear expectations and nurturing the relationships over time. It's crucial to remember that these support networks are not just about receiving help; they are also about giving back, supporting colleagues, and sharing the wisdom gained from experience. The creation of a strong, supportive community among political chaplains strengthens the profession as a whole, ensuring a higher standard of pastoral care and resilience within the demanding environment of political life. This mutual support helps prevent the isolation that often accompanies high-pressure roles and promotes a collaborative approach to professional development and self-care.

In conclusion, the construction of a comprehensive support network is not a supplementary aspect of the political chaplain's role; it is fundamental to its long-term sustainability and effectiveness. The combination of peer support, professional supervision, mentorship, spiritual direction, and dedicated time for personal reflection provides the necessary scaffolding for resilience, emotional well-being, and ethical decision-making within the challenging context of political life. The proactive cultivation of these relationships is not simply a matter of personal well-being; it is a vital component of providing responsible and effective pastoral care within a political landscape. The benefits extend beyond the individual chaplain,

strengthening the overall capacity of the profession and ensuring its continued contribution to the well-being of those served.

REFLECTION STEP

Please identify three networks to which you are currently connected and explain the reasons for your connection to each.

REFLECTION (CONTINUED)

CHAPTER 14
Professional Development and Continuing Education Opportunities

Building upon the foundation of self-care practices already discussed, the sustained effectiveness and well-being of a political chaplain hinges critically on a commitment to ongoing professional development and continuing education. This isn't simply about maintaining competency; it's about adapting to the ever-evolving landscape of political dynamics, refining pastoral skills, and deepening one's understanding of the intricate interplay between faith, politics, and community service. The demand for continuous learning in this multifaceted role is paramount. The unique challenges faced by political chaplains necessitate a proactive approach to professional growth, ensuring they remain equipped to navigate the complexities of their position effectively and ethically.

One of the most valuable avenues for professional development lies in participating in relevant workshops and conferences. Numerous organizations, both secular and faith-based, offer training programs specifically designed for chaplains, addressing various aspects of pastoral care, conflict resolution, and trauma-informed ministry. These workshops often provide opportunities for networking with other chaplains, sharing experiences, and learning from best practices employed in diverse contexts. Searching for keywords like "chaplaincy training," "pastoral care workshops," and "trauma-informed ministry" on professional development websites can yield a wealth of relevant options. Many theological seminaries and religious institutions also offer continuing education courses and workshops that address the specific needs of chaplains, incorporating relevant theological perspectives alongside practical skills.

Conferences focusing on political science, public policy, or community engagement can provide invaluable insights into the broader political context within which chaplains operate.

Attendance at such events allows for an expansion of understanding beyond the immediate concerns of pastoral care, fostering a more informed and nuanced approach to ministry within the political arena. These events provide exposure to current research, emerging trends, and policy debates, enriching the chaplain's capacity for insightful engagement with political leaders and community members alike. National and international organizations frequently host such conferences, offering diverse perspectives and valuable networking opportunities.

Moreover, specialized training programs catering to the unique needs of chaplains working within specific sectors, such as first responder support or crisis intervention, are invaluable. These programs equip chaplains with the specialized skills and knowledge required to effectively support individuals facing trauma or crisis situations. The ability to provide culturally sensitive and trauma-informed care is especially crucial in the politically charged environment, where emotional distress may be exacerbated by the complexities of political conflict. For instance, organizations focused on disaster relief or veteran support often offer comprehensive training for chaplains working in these areas, equipping them with the skills to effectively address the specific needs of these populations. Seeking out these specialized training opportunities ensures the chaplain remains equipped to offer the most effective and compassionate support.

Beyond formal workshops and conferences, accessing reputable online resources and scholarly publications is vital for continuous professional growth. Numerous journals dedicated to pastoral care, political science, and related fields publish cutting-edge research and insightful analyses that enrich the chaplain's understanding of

the dynamics at play. Furthermore, online courses and webinars offer flexible and accessible opportunities for continuous learning, adapting to the individual chaplain's schedule and learning preferences. These resources can address topics ranging from grief counseling to conflict mediation, providing an enhanced range of skills beneficial in the complex political landscape. Staying abreast of emerging trends in pastoral care is equally essential. The field of pastoral care is constantly evolving, with new approaches and methodologies emerging to address the changing needs of individuals and communities. Regularly engaging with professional journals, attending continuing education events, and actively participating in professional organizations help the chaplain stay current with the latest best practices. This ensures that the care provided remains relevant and effective, adapting to the diverse needs of individuals within the political community.

Furthermore, familiarity with recent research in fields such as psychology and sociology enhances the chaplain's ability to understand the complexities of human behavior and tailor their approach accordingly.

Furthermore, networking with colleagues and mentors plays a crucial role in professional development. Sharing experiences, discussing challenges, and seeking advice from experienced chaplains can provide invaluable support and guidance. Joining professional organizations related to chaplaincy, political science, or community service offers valuable opportunities for networking, collaboration, and access to resources and mentorship. Mentorship programs specifically designed for chaplains can be especially beneficial, providing guidance and support from seasoned professionals navigating similar challenges. These connections serve not only as sources of practical wisdom but also as crucial outlets for emotional support and shared understanding. Regular participation in professional networks enhances the capacity for

reflective practice, critical evaluation of one's own ministry, and the adoption of best practices from colleagues.

Finally, engaging in self-reflective practices is vital for sustained professional growth. Maintaining a reflective journal, regularly evaluating one's approach to ministry, and seeking supervision or feedback from trusted mentors or colleagues allows for continuous improvement and adaptation. This process of self-reflection ensures that chaplains remain attuned to their own strengths and limitations, actively seeking avenues for professional growth and refinement. The commitment to continual self-reflection ensures that the chaplain's ministry remains both ethical and effective, adapting to the complex demands of the political environment while upholding the highest standards of pastoral care. By combining the practical strategies of self-care with a commitment to continuous professional development, political chaplains can enhance their resilience, refine their skills, and effectively serve within the demanding context of political life. The journey of professional growth is ongoing, mirroring the continuous evolution of the political and societal landscape they serve.

REFLECTION STEP

My grandmother always said, "The biggest room is the room for improvement." List areas of your professional life where you want to grow.

REFLECTION (CONTINUED)

CHAPTER 15
Case Studies

Case Study 1 | Navigating a Conflict of Interest

The intricacies of navigating the intersection of faith, politics, and community service are vividly illustrated in the following case study. This real-life scenario, drawn from the Bahamian context, highlights the complex ethical dilemmas that can confront a political chaplain. The case involves a chaplain, whom we will refer to as Chaplain X, serving within a prominent political party in The Bahamas. Chaplain X, a respected figure known for unwavering commitment to the faith and the community, became entangled in a situation demanding careful consideration of ethical principles and the potential for conflict of interest.

The conflict arose during a period of intense political campaigning leading up to a crucial general election. A significant infrastructural project, proposed by the ruling party—the party Chaplain X served—promised to revitalize a marginalized community, but it also faced strong opposition from environmental groups and residents concerned about potential ecological damage. The proposed project involved the construction of a new port facility, crucial for economic development but potentially devastating to a nearby coral reef ecosystem.

Chaplain X, deeply committed to the well-being of the community being served, recognized the potential benefits of the project: increased employment opportunities, improved infrastructure, and enhanced economic prospects for a historically disadvantaged population. However, the chaplain also felt a strong moral obligation to consider the potential environmental consequences, particularly the potential damage to the delicate coral reef, a critical part of the

Bahamian ecosystem and a vital source of livelihood for many local fishing communities. The community's reaction was divided; some embraced the promise of economic prosperity while others prioritized the ecological preservation of their immediate environment.

The chaplain's dilemma was further complicated because of being the chaplain within the ruling party. While that role wasn't explicitly political in nature, a close relationship with party leadership and frequent attendance at party events presented the risk of the chaplain's views being interpreted as endorsements of the party's stance on the project. Remaining silent, however, could be interpreted as tacit approval, further complicating the chaplain's ethical position. The party leadership, eager to secure the project's approval, subtly pressured Chaplain X to publicly support their position, emphasizing the project's benefits and downplaying the environmental concerns.

Chaplain X grappled intensely with this internal conflict. The chaplain's faith emphasized stewardship of creation, a perspective that strongly resonated with the environmental concerns. Simultaneously, pastoral care responsibilities demanded attentiveness to the needs of the entire community, including those who saw the project as a path out of economic hardship. Chaplain X felt silence was not an option; the chaplain's conscience demanded an active role in guiding the community through this contentious issue.

The chaplain's decision-making process involved several crucial steps. **First,** Chaplain X sought counsel from trusted mentors and colleagues, both inside and outside of the political realm. These conversations helped clarify the ethical dimensions of the dilemma, reinforcing the importance of impartiality and transparency. This process highlighted the need for careful consideration of all perspectives, and it reinforced the understanding that the chaplain's faith required balancing commitments to justice and environmental stewardship with responsibility to the community being served.

Secondly, Chaplain X conducted thorough research, studying environmental impact assessment reports, engaging with environmental experts, and listening to the concerns of residents on both sides of the debate. This in-depth exploration allowed the formulation of a more informed and nuanced understanding of the situation, moving beyond the simplified narratives presented by either side of the political divide. It was a crucial step in making an informed and responsible decision. The careful gathering of information ensured the chaplain's response was founded on knowledge rather than assumptions or emotional reactions.

Thirdly, Chaplain X decided to take a public stance, albeit a cautious one, issuing a statement expressing deep concern for both the economic well-being of the community and the protection of the environment. The chaplain did not directly endorse or oppose the project but instead called for a comprehensive dialogue that involved all stakeholders: government officials, environmental experts, community members, and business leaders. The chaplain's statement emphasized the need for transparency, accountability, and a thorough assessment of the potential environmental impact before proceeding with the project.

The statement called for a collaborative process designed to create a solution that balanced the benefits of economic development with environmental protection. This approach demonstrated a commitment to serving the entire community, rather than aligning solely with the position of the ruling party. Chaplain X's commitment to impartiality and fairness was clear, illustrating the ability to navigate a challenging situation without compromising integrity.

The outcome of Chaplain X's actions was multifaceted. The public statement generated wider community discussion, leading to a more thorough review of the environmental impact assessment. While the project ultimately proceeded, significant modifications were implemented to mitigate the potential ecological damage.

These modifications included stricter environmental regulations, investment in reef restoration projects, and the establishment of a community oversight committee to monitor the project's impact.

The dialogue initiated by Chaplain X's stance fostered a sense of collaboration and trust among various stakeholders, showcasing the significant role faith leadership can play in bridging divides and advocating for responsible policy decisions.

This case study underscores the crucial role of integrity and impartiality in political chaplaincy. Chaplain X's actions demonstrated the ability to navigate a conflict of interest responsibly, prioritizing ethical considerations and community well-being over partisan loyalty. The experience demonstrated that maintaining a strong moral compass while serving within a political context is both challenging and critically important, and that an independent voice offering counsel based on deep engagement with all perspectives is a vital ingredient in promoting justice and the common good. It underscores the value of thoughtful deliberation, careful research, and a commitment to transparent dialogue in resolving complex ethical dilemmas. The successful navigation of this delicate situation reaffirms the potential for positive influence when faith-based leadership actively participates in public life, bringing ethical reflection and community-centered approaches to the political arena.

Moreover, this case study highlights the importance of self-reflection and the critical role of mentoring and peer support in maintaining ethical integrity within a demanding environment.

Chaplain X's ability to make a responsible decision stemmed not only from personal values but also from the guidance and support received from others. This emphasizes the importance of creating networks of support for political chaplains, fostering environments where open dialogue, constructive critique, and ethical reflection can flourish. Continuous professional development, coupled with regular reflection and peer support, are vital in equipping chaplains with the tools they must have to navigate the intricate ethical challenges inherent in their unique vocation.

In conclusion, the experience of Chaplain X offers valuable insights into the complexities of political chaplaincy in the Bahamian context. The case underscores the importance of ethical considerations, the value of careful decision-making processes, and the power of transparent dialogue in fostering constructive engagement within a political environment. It also demonstrates the importance of seeking advice from trusted mentors and colleagues, engaging in thorough research, and continuously reflecting on one's approach to ministry. Commitment to these principles is critical in maintaining integrity, building trust, and promoting the common good within the complex intersection of faith, politics, and community service. This case underscores the profound responsibility of political chaplains to serve as ethical guides, advocating for justice and the common good while navigating the often-challenging realities of the political landscape.

Case Study 2 | Providing Pastoral Care in a High-Stress Environment

This second case study shifts our focus from the complexities of navigating internal political conflicts to the immediate aftermath of a devastating natural disaster. Hurricane Dorian, in 2019, ravaged the Abaco Islands and Grand Bahama, leaving behind a trail of destruction and immense human suffering. In the immediate aftermath, the need for pastoral care transcended the usual parameters of political affiliation, demanding a response that prioritized the basic human needs of a traumatized population.

This case study examines the work of Chaplain Y, a chaplain affiliated with a non-governmental organization (NGO) operating in Grand Bahama. Chaplain Y, unlike Chaplain X, did not have a direct affiliation with any political party. However, the chaplain's work during and after the hurricane powerfully illustrated the intersection

between faith-based service, community resilience, and the indirect influence such service can have within the political sphere. The chaplain's work became intrinsically intertwined with the government's disaster relief efforts, even without direct political ties.

The immediate aftermath of Hurricane Dorian presented unprecedented challenges. Communication networks were severely disrupted, leaving many families separated and uncertain about the fate of their loved ones. Basic necessities such as food, water, and shelter were scarce, and the widespread destruction of homes and infrastructure left many in a state of shock and despair. The psychological toll on the survivors was profound, with high rates of trauma, anxiety, and depression reported.

Chaplain Y, along with a small team of volunteers, worked tirelessly in the devastated areas. Their initial response focused on providing immediate physical and emotional support. They distributed essential supplies, provided comfort and solace to those who had lost everything, and helped to reunite families separated by the storm. Their presence was a constant source of hope amidst the devastation. The work often involved navigating hazardous conditions, including damaged roads, collapsed buildings, and the ever-present threat of further storms.

The NGO's resources were quickly stretched thin, highlighting the inherent limitations of relying solely on volunteer efforts in the face of such a large-scale disaster. Chaplain Y, however, recognized the strategic importance of coordinating with government agencies and other NGOs to maximize their impact. This chaplain became a vital link, not only providing pastoral care but also assisting in the logistics of relief efforts by helping to identify vulnerable populations, assessing the extent of the damage, and facilitating communication between survivors and relief agencies.

One crucial aspect of Chaplain Y's work was the ability to bridge the gap between the government's disaster relief efforts and the immediate needs of the community. This chaplain acted as an intermediary, translating government policies into accessible information for survivors and relaying the concerns of the community to government officials. This role became increasingly important as the initial emergency response transitioned into long-term recovery efforts. In this process, Chaplain Y exemplified the crucial function of a trusted community leader, ensuring transparency and fostering trust during a time of immense uncertainty and vulnerability.

A significant challenge faced by Chaplain Y was the overwhelming scale of human suffering. The sheer number of traumatized individuals and the depth of their emotional distress took a toll on the chaplain and the team. Burnout became a very real threat, demanding a constant awareness of personal limits and a proactive approach to self-care. This involved implementing strategies such as regular debriefing sessions, ensuring access to peer support, and prioritizing personal mental and physical health. The case study underscores the vital importance of providing support for those providing support—a key element often overlooked in discussions of disaster relief.

Moreover, Chaplain Y encountered ethical dilemmas related to resource allocation. The limited resources available necessitated difficult decisions about who received priority access to essential supplies and services. This involved navigating complex factors such as age, health status, and the extent of damage suffered.

Chaplain Y's approach was guided by principles of fairness and equity, prioritizing those in most immediate need and ensuring a transparent distribution process. This aspect of the work highlights the necessity of well-defined ethical guidelines within disaster relief operations, providing a framework for difficult decisions and fostering community trust.

The case study also highlights the long-term impact of the hurricane and the ongoing need for pastoral care. Months and years after the storm, the psychological and emotional wounds lingered, necessitating continued support for survivors. Chaplain Y and the accompanying team provided long-term counseling, facilitated community healing initiatives, and supported the rebuilding of social networks. This demonstrated the significant role that faith-based organizations can play in fostering resilience and promoting long-term recovery in the wake of a disaster.

The interaction between Chaplain Y and political entities wasn't direct, but it was profoundly significant. The NGO's work, heavily reliant on Chaplain Y's community leadership, provided invaluable insights into the effectiveness of different relief strategies, informing government policy and resource allocation. This highlights the subtle yet powerful influence of faith-based service on the political landscape, showing how community-level work can influence broader policy discussions and improve the efficacy of governmental responses to disaster. The data gathered through the chaplain's community work, even though informally collected, provided valuable real-world feedback, shaping the long-term recovery plans.

The experience of Chaplain Y in the wake of Hurricane Dorian provides a powerful counterpoint to the complexities of the political environment explored in the previous case study. While Chaplain X navigated the intricate ethical considerations within the political sphere, Chaplain Y demonstrated the profound impact of faith-based service in a crisis, highlighting the important role of community leadership in disaster response. Both case studies underscore the importance of ethical decision-making, the value of community engagement, and the critical need for self-care within the challenging context of political chaplaincy and disaster relief. The combined impact showcases the multifaceted nature of chaplaincy, its diverse roles, and the enduring need for ethical leadership in both political and humanitarian settings. The resilience of the community, aided by compassionate leaders like Chaplain Y, is a testament to the power of faith and collaborative community action in the face of adversity. The chaplain's work serves as a beacon of hope and inspiration, highlighting the essential role of pastoral care in the healing process and the lasting influence of faith-based leadership within a recovering community. This highlights the need for ongoing support and training for those who provide pastoral care in high-stress environments, ensuring they possess the skills and resources to navigate the complexities of such challenging circumstances.

This role extends beyond immediate crisis management to encompass long-term community recovery and resilience building. The actions of Chaplain Y serve as a reminder that the impact of pastoral care can be profoundly transformative, shaping not only individual lives but also the trajectory of entire communities. The future of political chaplaincy requires a multi-pronged approach to enhancing its effectiveness and addressing its challenges.

Firstly, there is a need for increased professionalization of the field. This includes developing standardized training programs that equip chaplains with the necessary skills in conflict resolution, community engagement, ethical decision-making, and self-care. Professional certification, overseen by a relevant governing body, could enhance credibility and ensure a certain level of competency within the field. Establishing mentorship programs, where experienced chaplains guide and support newcomers, would also be invaluable. The establishment of professional associations or networks for political chaplains can foster collaboration, knowledge-sharing, and support amongst practitioners. Such organizations could play a crucial role in setting ethical guidelines, promoting best practices, and providing professional development opportunities.

Secondly, more research is needed to understand the specific challenges and best practices in different political contexts. The Bahamian context, for example, presents unique challenges and opportunities that may not be applicable in other countries.

Comparative studies examining political chaplaincy in diverse settings would contribute significantly to the field's knowledge base, fostering the development of adaptable and effective strategies.

Research should focus on exploring the effectiveness of different chaplaincy models, the impact on community well-being, and the long-term sustainability of these roles within the ever-evolving political landscape. Qualitative research methods, such as interviews and case studies, could offer rich insights into the lived experiences of political chaplains and the communities they serve.

Thirdly, ongoing dialogue and collaboration between political leaders, religious institutions, and community organizations are crucial. This collaborative approach would foster a shared understanding of the role and responsibilities of political chaplains, ensuring that their work aligns with the broader needs of the community and the political system. Regular consultations and joint initiatives would strengthen the integration of chaplaincy services into the fabric of society, creating a supportive ecosystem for chaplains to thrive and serve effectively. Such collaborations could also lead to the development of policies and resources that support the work of political chaplains, fostering a more sustainable and impactful role within the political landscape.

In conclusion, the case studies presented have provided valuable insights into the complexities and rewards of political chaplaincy. The lessons learned highlight the need for ethical leadership, strong community engagement, and robust self-care strategies. Looking toward the future, enhancing professionalization, expanding research, and fostering collaboration are crucial steps in strengthening the field and ensuring its continued relevance in an increasingly polarized and complex world. The goal is to create a landscape where political chaplains can effectively serve both political leaders and the wider community, fostering healing, reconciliation, and positive social change. The path forward requires a commitment to ongoing learning, adaptation, and a steadfast dedication to the principles of ethical leadership, community service, and self-care. Only through such a multifaceted approach can political chaplaincy achieve its full potential in contributing to a more just, compassionate, and resilient society.

CHAPTER 16
Summary of Key Findings and Implications

This book, *Politics and Chaplaincy,* has explored the intricate relationship between faith, politics, and community service, specifically within the unique context of The Bahamas. The preceding chapters have probed into the historical evolution of this intersection, examining the distinct roles and responsibilities of political chaplains compared to their pastoral counterparts. We've analyzed two case studies, showcasing the diverse challenges and remarkable successes encountered by individuals navigating this demanding vocation. The narratives presented offer a rich tapestry of experiences, revealing both the profound potential for positive impact and the inherent difficulties in balancing political allegiance with broader community needs.

In summary, this book has provided an exploration of political chaplaincy in The Bahamian context, highlighting the unique challenges and remarkable potential of this often-overlooked vocation. The key findings underscore the indispensable importance of ethical leadership, active community engagement, and robust self-care strategies. The future of this field demands a commitment to ongoing professionalization, expanded research, and strengthened collaboration among stakeholders. Only through such a multifaceted approach can political chaplaincy achieve its full potential, contributing significantly to a more just, compassionate, and resilient society. The journey ahead requires unwavering dedication to the principles of ethical leadership, unwavering community service, and steadfast prioritization of self-care—a crucial foundation for long-term effectiveness and positive impact. The hope is that this work will serve as a valuable resource for political chaplains, aspiring chaplains, and those seeking a deeper understanding of this vital intersection of faith, politics, and community service.

Recommendations for Future Research and Practice

The preceding chapters have laid bare the complexities and nuances of political chaplaincy in The Bahamas, highlighting both the remarkable potential and the significant challenges inherent in this unique vocation. While we've examined existing practices and explored diverse case studies, significant opportunities remain for further research and the refinement of best practices within this crucial field. This section outlines key recommendations for future research and practice, designed to enhance the effectiveness, sustainability, and ethical integrity of political chaplaincy, not only in The Bahamas, but potentially serving as a model for other contexts globally.

One of the most pressing needs is a comprehensive, longitudinal study examining the long-term impact of political chaplaincy on community relations. While we've explored individual instances of positive community impact, a more systematic investigation is required to assess the sustained effects of various chaplaincy approaches on key social indicators, such as conflict resolution rates, levels of social cohesion, and perceptions of trust in political institutions. This study should employ mixed-methods research, incorporating quantitative data analysis to measure tangible outcomes alongside qualitative data—through interviews and focus groups— to capture the nuanced perspectives of community members and political stakeholders. Such a study could delve into the effectiveness of chaplain-led initiatives promoting reconciliation, mediating disputes, or facilitating community dialogue. It would also be crucial to investigate how the presence of a political chaplain influences the trust and engagement of diverse communities, encompassing both religious and secular populations. Identifying specific, measurable outcomes would allow for greater accountability and contribute to a more evidence-based understanding of the value added by political chaplains.

Further research is needed to evaluate the effectiveness of diverse pastoral care approaches within the context of political chaplaincy. While the spiritual guidance provided by chaplains forms a crucial aspect of their role, the application of these approaches within a highly charged political environment requires careful consideration. This necessitates a comparative study examining different pastoral care models and their efficacy in addressing the specific needs of political leaders, first responders, and the wider community. The study could analyze various counseling techniques, conflict resolution strategies, and community engagement approaches, assessing their suitability within the political context and their ability to foster resilience, promote well-being, and facilitate positive social change. This research might explore the use of trauma-informed care for first responders dealing with stressful situations, the development of tailored programs addressing the specific psychological demands of political life, and the use of spiritual practices to foster empathy and understanding amongst individuals with differing political viewpoints. Such a comparative approach would ultimately contribute to the development of best practices tailored to the unique needs of this setting.

Developing a robust framework of best practices for political chaplaincy is crucial. This requires a multi-faceted approach, drawing from both empirical research and the wisdom of experienced practitioners. A collaborative project involving political chaplains, religious leaders, political scientists, and ethicists could lead to the creation of guidelines addressing ethical dilemmas, professional standards, and community engagement strategies. These guidelines could be disseminated through training programs, mentorship initiatives, and professional networks, fostering a culture of accountability and continuous improvement. The framework

should incorporate elements such as conflict-of-interest protocols, guidelines on maintaining impartiality, strategies for balancing political allegiance with community service, and recommendations for effective communication and relationship building. Specific modules addressing the use of social media in political chaplaincy, the ethical considerations of offering counsel to political leaders, and methods for navigating potential power imbalances are also critical. This comprehensive framework would provide a valuable resource for both seasoned professionals and those entering the field, ensuring a higher standard of practice and enhanced public trust. The role of self-care within political chaplaincy warrants further investigation. The emotional toll of working in such a high-pressure environment cannot be underestimated. Therefore, research examining the effectiveness of various self-care strategies and support systems is critical. This could involve qualitative studies interviewing political chaplains about their self-care practices, the resources they find most helpful, and the challenges they face in maintaining their well-being. The findings could inform the development of tailored programs offering peer support, mentorship, and access to mental health professionals specializing in the unique stressors faced by those in this profession. The exploration of mindfulness practices, stress-reduction techniques, and spiritual practices designed to enhance resilience, and emotional well-being should also be integral to this research. Developing a comprehensive support network and promoting a culture that prioritizes self-care are essential for the long-term sustainability of political chaplaincy.

Beyond the Bahamian context, comparative studies examining political chaplaincy in diverse geopolitical environments are needed. Analyzing the similarities and differences in the role and function of political chaplains across varying cultural, religious, and political systems can provide invaluable insights. This research should explore how cultural contexts influence the interpretation of religious principles in the political sphere and how the role of a chaplain adapts to different power structures. By studying diverse settings, we can glean lessons and best practices that can enhance the effectiveness of political chaplaincy in a wider range of contexts. A global perspective can enrich our understanding of the challenges and successes of this multifaceted vocation.

Finally, collaboration between relevant stakeholders is key. This includes establishing ongoing dialogues between government agencies, religious institutions, first responder organizations, and community leaders. These discussions can foster a shared understanding of the role and contributions of political chaplains, leading to the development of supportive policies and resources. This collaborative approach should focus on creating a framework for formal recognition and professionalization of political chaplaincy, fostering a climate of collaboration and respect within the profession.

In conclusion, this chapter has only scratched the surface of the significant potential for growth and development within the field of political chaplaincy. The recommendations outlined above represent crucial steps toward a more formalized, effective, and ethically sound practice, ensuring that the invaluable contributions of political chaplains are both recognized and optimized. Through focused research and strengthened collaborations, we can pave the way for a more impactful and enduring role for political chaplains in fostering social harmony, promoting ethical leadership, and supporting communities in navigating the complex challenges of the political landscape.

CHAPTER 17
Ethical Guidelines and Codes of Conduct

Ethical considerations form the bedrock of effective and responsible political chaplaincy. Navigating the complex interplay between faith, politics, and community requires a robust ethical framework, guiding actions and decisions in a way that upholds integrity, promotes fairness, and prioritizes the well-being of all involved. This section outlines key ethical guidelines and codes of conduct, offering practical examples to illustrate their application in diverse scenarios.

At the heart of ethical political chaplaincy lies the principle of **integrity**. This entails unwavering honesty, transparency, and consistency in actions and words. A political chaplain must act with sincerity, avoiding any form of deception or manipulation, even when under pressure to conform to partisan interests. This commitment to truthfulness extends to all interactions, from public pronouncements to private conversations. For instance, a chaplain might be pressured by a political party to endorse a particular policy or candidate that conflicts with their personal conscience or religious beliefs. Maintaining integrity in this situation necessitates a careful and honest approach, potentially involving open dialogue with party leadership, a clear articulation of one's ethical limitations, or even a decision to withdraw from the role if the conflict becomes irreconcilable. The value of transparency is paramount; concealing information or engaging in behind-the-scenes maneuvering would compromise this crucial principle.

Closely related to integrity is the principle of **impartiality**. While a chaplain may be associated with a particular political party or ideology, a chaplain's role demands a commitment to serving all members of the community, regardless of their political affiliations. This doesn't necessitate neutrality on all issues—chaplains retain the right to express their personal views—but it does require that they avoid favoritism or discrimination in their pastoral care and community engagement. Imagine a scenario where a chaplain provides counseling services to individuals from both the ruling and opposition parties. Impartiality demands that they offer the same level of care, empathy, and support to each individual, without letting political allegiances influence their professional judgment. Showing partiality toward one group over another could damage trust, hinder their ability to serve their community effectively, and potentially undermine the integrity of the chaplaincy role itself. This impartiality needs to be actively demonstrated through consistent behavior and a demonstrable commitment to equitable treatment for all.

The principle of **responsible leadership** guides the actions of political chaplains in interactions with both political figures and the wider community. This includes the responsible use of power and influence, avoiding the temptation to exploit their position for personal gain or to advance partisan agendas. Chaplains are expected to act as ethical role models, embodying values of service, humility, and respect. For example, a chaplain might be approached by a politician seeking advice on a sensitive matter involving the community. Responsible leadership necessitates providing guidance based on ethical principles, even if this might involve challenging the politician's perspective or recommending a course of action that might be unpopular. Furthermore, a chaplain might be in a position to influence policy decisions. In this case, responsible leadership requires transparently articulating values and concerns, acting as an advocate for the voiceless, and ensuring that all policy considerations account for the broader impact on society and reflect ethical principles.

A further crucial ethical consideration is **confidentiality**. Political chaplains often encounter sensitive information during their interactions with individuals seeking spiritual guidance or emotional support. Maintaining strict confidentiality is essential, protecting the privacy and vulnerability of those who trust them. Exceptions might exist only under legally mandated circumstances, such as when there is a credible threat of imminent harm to oneself or others. Transparency on the limitations of confidentiality—particularly the potential for mandatory reporting—builds a foundation of trust. This is particularly relevant when dealing with issues such as domestic violence, substance abuse, or suicidal ideation, where legal requirements necessitate breaking confidentiality to ensure safety and well-being.

The ethical obligations of political chaplains also extend to **conflict of interest**. Avoiding situations where personal interests conflict with professional responsibilities is paramount. This could involve declining gifts or favors from political figures, refraining from engaging in partisan political activities outside the chaplaincy role, or refusing to endorse candidates or policies they believe are ethically problematic. Situations demanding careful navigation might involve requests for financial contributions or endorsements. Transparency and adherence to established guidelines for avoiding conflict of interest are critical for maintaining the integrity and credibility of the role. The importance of establishing clear boundaries between personal and professional roles cannot be overstated.

Code of Conduct: While no single universally accepted code of conduct exists specifically for political chaplains, adapting existing codes from organizations like the International Fellowship of Chaplains (ifoc.org) provides a valuable framework. This framework needs to be further adapted to reflect the specific cultural, political, and religious context of The Bahamas, incorporating relevant

Bahamian laws and customs. Such a local code should explicitly address issues unique to the Bahamian political landscape, such as the strong ties between religion and politics in the nation. The code must clearly articulate expectations regarding impartiality, conflict of interest, confidentiality, and responsible leadership within this specific context.

The development and implementation of a robust ethical framework and code of conduct for political chaplains in The Bahamas are crucial for fostering trust, promoting responsible leadership, and ensuring that this unique vocation remains accountable to both religious and civic standards. The continued dialogue amongst religious leaders, political figures, and community members is essential to creating and refining such a framework, ensuring its relevance and effectiveness in serving the broader community. Regular training and ethical reflection sessions will be paramount in fostering ongoing adherence to the code and developing ethical decision-making abilities within this challenging and rewarding field. Ongoing review and amendment of the code will ensure its continued relevance and adaptability to the changing political and social landscape.

Acknowledgments

This book would not have been possible without the generous support and guidance of many individuals. Their willingness to be vulnerable and honest is a testament to their dedication to their calling. I am especially indebted to Chaplain Raymond K. Wells, Chief Chaplain of the Royal Bahamas Defence Force, and Bahamas Regional Commander for Frontline Chaplains International, whose contributions were invaluable.

Finally, my heartfelt thanks to my wife Shena and our family and church for their patience, understanding, and unwavering encouragement. Their love and support provided the strength and resilience needed to complete this project.

Glossary

Political Chaplain: A chaplain who provides spiritual and pastoral care within the political sphere, often serving a political party, government officials, or legislative bodies.

First Responder: Personnel who are among the first to arrive and provide assistance at the scene of an emergency, including police officers, firefighters, paramedics, and emergency medical technicians.

Pastoral Care: The provision of spiritual and emotional support to individuals and communities, often through counseling, prayer, and other forms of spiritual guidance.

Chaplains in Parliament and Senate: Those who offer spiritual guidance and support to members of the legislature and their staff. They provide a confidential space for reflection and prayer, regardless of faith background, and often lead in opening ceremonies or offer pastoral care during times of stress or crisis. Their roles are primarily pastoral, offering comfort and support, rather than legislative or political involvement. They act as a neutral presence, fostering a sense of community and well-being within the often-intense political environment.

About the Author

Jonathan is an Assemblies of God USA Commissioned Emergency Services Chaplain with Advanced Ecclesiastical Endorsement from The Assemblies of God Commission on Chaplains. He serves as the Lead Pastor of Glad Tidings Tabernacle, the Caribbean Regional Commander for Frontline Chaplains International, and a Chaplain Coordinator for The Billy Graham Rapid Response Team.

He focuses on equipping first responders and chaplains with the spiritual and practical tools necessary to succeed in their roles. In recognition of his work as a chaplain and first responder in the United States, Jonathan received the U.S. President's Lifetime Achievement Award for Community Service and Volunteerism in 2023.

Jonathan has experience in non-fiction writing and aims to share messages related to chaplaincy and leadership with a global audience. Jonathan lives in Key West, Florida, with his family.

For more information, visit **CAREYPRESS.ORG.**

PAST COMMUNITY INVOLVEMENT

In 1993, Dr. Carey founded Programme S.U.R.E. (Success Ultimately Reassures Everyone) Genesis Academy, a public alternative school in Grand Bahama Island, The Bahamas, supporting students with disciplinary challenges. He served as principal for six years.

Jonathan has also been a member of The Bahamas National Crime Commission, chaired the Bahamas National Youth Advisory Board, and directed the West Grand Bahama Community Tourism Board under The Ministry of Tourism.

PRESENT COMMUNITY INVOLVEMENT

Founder of Project Ruth, Dominican Republic

The fundamental principles of PR's strategy involve establishing a collaborative relationship with government officials and leaders of the Christian community to:

- *Reset getaways for national First Responders and their spouses.*

- *Undergird the educational system.* We currently provide classroom space and support programs for fifty public school students.

- *Teach the love of Jesus and social values.* Through our local church ministries and short-term mission trips, we teach by example.

- *Provide healthcare services.* Our partnership with the government provides the only healthcare services available to 4,000 residents in La Florida, San Juan de la Maguana, Dominican Republic.

Board Member at Won by One to Jamaica

Won by One to Jamaica empowers individuals by fostering genuine connections and providing valuable resources through education, medical, economic, and spiritual initiatives.

Advisory Board Member, Juvenile Justice Circuit #16

The mission of the Florida Department of Juvenile Justice is to enhance public safety through high-quality, effective services for youth and families delivered by world-class professionals dedicated to building a stronger, safer Florida.

DAILY
GOSPEL
NETWORK
STEPS TO SUCCESS
WATCH
On
tv
Roku TV
amazon fireTV
DGN Plus: 10:30AM EST SATURDAY
Jonathan Carey
ALSO AVAILABLE ON
www.dailygospelnetwork.tv